First World War
and Army of Occupation
War Diary
France, Belgium and Germany

41 DIVISION
Divisional Troops
Royal Army Medical Corps
140 Field Ambulance
5 May 1916 - 31 October 1917

WO95/2630/1

The Naval & Military Press Ltd
www.nmarchive.com
Published in association with The National Archives

Published by

The Naval & Military Press Ltd

Unit 10 Ridgewood Industrial Park,

Uckfield, East Sussex,

TN22 5QE England

Tel: +44 (0) 1825 749494

www.naval-military-press.com

www.nmarchive.com

This diary has been reprinted in facsimile from the original. Any imperfections are inevitably reproduced and the quality may fall short of modern type and cartographic standards.

© Crown Copyright
Images reproduced by permission of The National Archives, London, England, 2015.

Contents

Document type	Place/Title	Date From	Date To
Heading	WO95/2630/1 May 1916-Oct 1917 140 Field Ambulance		
Heading	41st Division 140th Field Ambulance May 1916-Oct 1917 Mar 1918-1919 Oct To Rhine Garrison Italy 1917 Nov-1918 Feb		
Heading	41th Div CB 140 F.A. May 1916		
War Diary	Farnborough	05/05/1916	05/05/1916
War Diary	Southampton	05/05/1916	05/05/1916
War Diary	Havre	06/05/1916	06/05/1916
War Diary	Sanvic	06/05/1916	06/05/1916
War Diary	Havre	07/05/1916	07/05/1916
War Diary	Steenvercq	08/05/1916	08/05/1916
War Diary	Ebblinghem	08/05/1916	09/05/1916
War Diary	Burre	09/05/1916	15/05/1916
War Diary	Strazeele	16/05/1916	29/05/1916
Heading	DAG Base		
Heading	S/June 1916 C/O 140 F.A.		
War Diary	La Creche	01/06/1916	01/06/1916
War Diary	Pont de Nieppe	01/06/1916	30/06/1916
Miscellaneous	W. 188 S.324.		
Miscellaneous			
Heading	War Diary of 140th Field Ambulance Volume 3 July 1916		
War Diary	Pont de Nieppe	02/07/1916	31/07/1916
Miscellaneous			
War Diary	Pont de Nieppe	05/08/1916	18/08/1916
War Diary	Meteren	19/08/1916	22/08/1916
War Diary	Bailleul West Station.	23/08/1916	23/08/1916
War Diary	Pont Remy	23/08/1916	23/08/1916
War Diary	Eaucourt	24/08/1916	31/08/1916
Miscellaneous	Programme of Training for One Week-Commanding Saturday August 26 1916 Appendix 3		
Miscellaneous	Appendix 4.		
Heading	War Diary of 140th Field Amb 41st Division from 1st September to 30th September 1916 (Volume V)		
War Diary	Eaucourt	01/09/1916	07/09/1916
War Diary	Longpre les Corps Saints	07/09/1916	07/09/1916
War Diary	Mericourt Camp E9 62D.Nr Albert	07/09/1916	09/09/1916
War Diary	Camp Nr Becordel	09/09/1916	10/09/1916
War Diary	Bellevue Fme Albert	10/09/1916	11/09/1916
War Diary	Bellevue Fme	12/09/1916	14/09/1916
War Diary	Green. Dump SW of Lon Gueval	15/09/1916	15/09/1916
War Diary	Green Dump	15/09/1916	16/09/1916
War Diary	Crucifix S of Longueval	16/09/1916	16/09/1916
War Diary	Crucifix or Shrine	17/09/1916	17/09/1916
War Diary	Crucifix	17/09/1916	18/09/1916
War Diary	Camp E Albert Sheet 62D E15a7.6	18/09/1916	23/09/1916
War Diary	Camp E Albert	24/09/1916	30/09/1916
Miscellaneous	140th Field Ambulance Operation Order No. 5 app 4.	10/09/1916	10/09/1916
Operation(al) Order(s)	140th Field Ambulance Operation Order No. 6. app 5		

Miscellaneous	September		
Heading	Duplicate Medical War Diary 140th Diary 14th Field Amb. 41st Div.		
War Diary	Camp E Albert	01/10/1916	03/10/1916
War Diary	Camp at X29 d.4.5. on Mametz-Bazentin Road	04/10/1916	04/10/1916
War Diary	Camp X29.	05/10/1916	07/10/1916
War Diary	Camp X29 13.	07/10/1916	09/10/1916
War Diary	Camp X29d Medical Dump.	09/10/1916	10/10/1916
War Diary	Camp X29J.	11/10/1916	11/10/1916
War Diary	Becordel XV Corps Collecting Station Walieing Wounded.	12/10/1916	13/10/1916
War Diary	Becordel	14/10/1916	15/10/1916
War Diary	Ribemont	16/10/1916	16/10/1916
War Diary	Bettencourt	17/10/1916	19/10/1916
War Diary	Longpre State Meteren	20/10/1916	20/10/1916
War Diary	Meteren	20/10/1916	21/10/1916
War Diary	Boeschepe	21/10/1916	23/10/1916
War Diary	Boescheppe	24/10/1916	24/10/1916
War Diary	Reninghelst	24/10/1916	31/10/1916
Miscellaneous	October 1916		
Heading	War Diary of 140th Field Ambulance November 1916 Volume VII		
Heading	A.D.M.S. 41st Division		
War Diary	Reninghelst	01/11/1916	30/11/1916
Miscellaneous	November 1916 Appendix 7		
Miscellaneous	C27. A.D.M.S.	01/12/1916	01/12/1916
Heading	War Diary of 140th Field Ambulance from 1st Decr 16 to 31st Dec 16 Volume VIII		
War Diary	Reninghelst	01/12/1916	31/12/1916
Miscellaneous	A.D.M.S.	01/01/1917	01/01/1917
Miscellaneous	December 1916 Appendix 8 Appendix 8		
Heading	War Diary 140th Field Ambulance R.A.M.C. From Jan 1st 1917 To Jan 31st 1917		
War Diary	Reninghelst	01/01/1917	08/01/1917
War Diary	Wippenhoek	09/01/1917	31/01/1917
Operation(al) Order(s)	140th Field Ambulance Operation Order No 14. Appendix 8	06/01/1917	06/01/1917
Operation(al) Order(s)	140 Field Ambulance Operation Order No. 15 Appendix 9	08/01/1917	08/01/1917
Operation(al) Order(s)	Operation Order No. 16 Appendix 10	30/01/1917	30/01/1917
Miscellaneous	Appendix II		
Heading	War Diary 140th Field Ambulance from 1/2/17 To 28/2/17		
War Diary	Wippenhoek	01/02/1917	28/02/1917
Miscellaneous	Appendix 12.		
Heading	War Diary 140th Field Ambulance from 1st March 1917 To 31st March 1917		
War Diary	Wippenhoek	01/03/1917	31/03/1917
Miscellaneous	App 13		
Heading	War Diary 140th Field Ambulance R.A.M.C. From April 1st 1917 To April 30th 1917		
War Diary	Wittenhoek	01/04/1917	06/04/1917
War Diary	Steenvoorde	07/04/1917	07/04/1917
War Diary	Noordpene	07/04/1917	08/04/1917
War Diary	Eperlecques	08/04/1917	23/04/1917
War Diary	Nordpene	24/04/1917	24/04/1917

War Diary	Nordpene	24/04/1917	25/04/1917
War Diary	Camp Kemmel Road. M6a.8.8.	25/04/1917	30/04/1917
Operation(al) Order(s)	140 Field Ambulance Operation Order No. 17 Appendix 14.	03/04/1917	03/04/1917
Miscellaneous			
Operation(al) Order(s)	140 Field Ambulance Operation Order No. 18	05/04/1917	05/04/1917
Operation(al) Order(s)	140 Field Ambulance. Operation Order No 19 Appendix 16	06/04/1917	06/04/1917
Operation(al) Order(s)	140 Field Ambulance Operation Order No. 20 Appendix 17		
Miscellaneous	Programme for Training. Appendix 18		
Miscellaneous	of Field Ambulance		
Miscellaneous	Programme of Training		
Miscellaneous	of Field Ambulance		
Operation(al) Order(s)	140th Field Ambulance Operation Order No. 21 Appendix 19	22/04/1917	22/04/1917
Operation(al) Order(s)	140th Field Ambulance Operation Order No. 22. Appendix 20	23/04/1917	23/04/1917
Operation(al) Order(s)	140 Field Ambulance Operation Order No 23. Appendix 21	24/04/1917	24/04/1917
Miscellaneous	Yossues to the 140 Fd. Amb. for 1 year.		
Heading	War Diary 140th Field Ambulance R.A.M.C. From 1st May 1917 To 31st May 1917		
War Diary	Camp. Kemmel Road M6 a. 8.8.	01/05/1917	20/05/1917
War Diary	Camp. La Clytte Road M6 a.8.8.	20/05/1917	31/05/1917
Miscellaneous	Appendix No 23.		
Miscellaneous	Appendix 26		
Heading	War Diary 140th Field Ambulance R.A.M.C. From 1/6/17 To 30/6/17		
War Diary	La Clytte Rd M.D.S.	01/06/1917	08/06/1917
War Diary	Xth Corps M.D.S. La Clytte Rd	08/06/1917	13/06/1917
War Diary	M.D.S. La Clytte Rd M 6 A 8.8.	14/06/1917	24/06/1917
War Diary	M.D.S. V D.A.G. La Clytte Rd M. 6.A.8.8.	25/06/1917	28/06/1917
War Diary	Camp X 16.D.8.9.	30/06/1917	30/06/1917
Heading	War Diary 140th Field Ambulance R.A.M.C. From 1st July 1917 To 31st July 1917		
War Diary	Camp X. at X 16 D.8.8 Sheet 27 "B" Series	01/07/1917	13/07/1917
War Diary	Camp 8. at X.16.D.8.8.	14/07/1917	17/07/1917
War Diary	Conquerors Camp Westoutre Reninghelst Rd.	18/07/1917	23/07/1917
War Diary	Conqueror Camp.	24/07/1917	25/07/1917
War Diary	Chippawa Camp La Clytte Rd	26/07/1917	31/07/1917
Heading	War Diary 140th Field Ambulance R.A.M.C. from 1st August 1917 To 31st August 1917		
Heading	140 Field Ambulance War Diary August 1917		
War Diary	Chippawa MDS La Clytte Rd	01/08/1917	14/08/1917
War Diary	W.6.C.3.9 (Fletre Sheet 27)	15/08/1917	16/08/1917
War Diary	Camp. W 5.C.3.9. (Flatre Sheet 27)	18/08/1917	20/08/1917
War Diary	N.30.	20/08/1917	21/08/1917
War Diary	La Wattine (Sheet 27 S.E.)	21/08/1917	31/08/1917
Heading	War Diary of 140 Field Ambulance for September 1917 Vol 17		
War Diary	La Wattine	01/09/1917	14/09/1917
War Diary	Wallon Capelle	14/09/1917	14/09/1917
War Diary	Fletre	15/09/1917	15/09/1917
War Diary	Veerstraat	16/09/1917	17/09/1917
War Diary	Voormezele	18/09/1917	21/09/1917

War Diary	Lock 8	22/09/1917	23/09/1917
War Diary	Voormezele	22/09/1917	24/09/1917
War Diary	Caestre (Q 33. b Central)	25/09/1917	28/09/1917
War Diary	Ghyvelde	28/09/1917	30/09/1917
Diagram etc	Diagram Showing Line Of Evacuation Of Casualties.		
Operation(al) Order(s)	Operation Orders 140 Field Ambulance	19/09/1917	19/09/1917
Operation(al) Order(s)	140th Field Ambulance Operation Order No. 7	14/09/1916	14/09/1916
Miscellaneous	Re Division Of Area For Blast Distribution To 5 Sea Map		
Operation(al) Order(s)	140th Field Ambulance Operation Order No. 8.	03/10/1916	03/10/1916
Operation(al) Order(s)	140th Field Ambulance Operation Order No. 9.		
Operation(al) Order(s)	140th Field Ambulance Operation Order No. 10.		
Operation(al) Order(s)	140th Field Ambulance Operation Order No. 11. Corps Collecting Station For Walking Wounded		
Operation(al) Order(s)	140th Field Ambulance Operation Order No. 12	18/10/1916	18/10/1916
Operation(al) Order(s)	140th Field Ambulance Operation Order No. 13.	22/10/1916	22/10/1916
Heading	War Diary 140 Field Ambulance October 1917 Vol 18		
War Diary	Ghyvelde	01/10/1917	07/10/1917
War Diary	De Groote Kwinte Farm	07/10/1917	13/10/1917
War Diary	St Idesbalde	13/10/1917	29/10/1917
War Diary	Fort Mardick	29/10/1917	31/10/1917

1/ WO95/2630

May 1916 – Oct 1917

140 Field Ambulance

41ST DIVISION

140TH FIELD AMBULANCE

MAY 1916 - ~~DEC 1918~~ OCT 1917
MAR 1918 — 1919 OCT

TO RHINE GARRISON

ITALY 1917 NOV — 1918 FEB

Army Form C. 2118

140 F Amb

VOL I

WAR DIARY
or
INTELLIGENCE SUMMARY
(Erase heading not required.)

Place	Date	Hour	Summary of Events and Information	Remarks and references to Appendices
FARNBOROUGH	May 5	7.15 am	Entrained 1st Railroad in 20 minutes	
		8.15	2nd " " " " in advanced time	
SOUTHAMPTON		11 am	all embarked on board SS HT "INVENTOR"	
		7.30 pm	Sailed	
HAVRE	6	4.30 am	arrived	
		12.45 pm	Started disembarkation	
		5.20 pm	finished disembarkation	
SANVIC		7.45 pm	arrived at Rest Camp, raining	
	7		many casualties en route – one rest (?ami exchanged) – one rest't collar exchanged	
HAVRE	7	5 pm	Entrained with whole unit & about 250 infantry details. 50 carriages on trucks	
		7.30 pm	Entrainment completed, left HAVRE	
STEENVOORDE	8	4.30 pm	detrained – in 40 minutes with station clear	
ERBLINGHEM		5 to	arrived CHATEAU EBBLINGHEM	
	9	9.45 am	left Eberbg-Ham	
BOARE		3.15 pm	arrived billets BOARE (5 km)	
	10		unpacked kits – busy with sanitation	
	11	11 am	Practical demonstration to unit in "gas attack" chlorine & sulyl bromide	
	12		1st & 2nd Section went up to 28th F amb at PONT DE NIEPPE for instruction in the line	
			walk fine	
	13		very wet	
	14		Returned from PONT DE NIEPPE fine	

RDM

WAR DIARY or INTELLIGENCE SUMMARY

Army Form C. 2118

(Erase heading not required.)

Place	Date	Hour	Summary of Events and Information	Remarks and references to Appendices
STRAZEELE	Mar 16	7.15 am	Passed into STRAZEELE (from) Sgt Loffland & 30 Mor-5 when to 28th Fld Amb for instruction.	
"	17		Fine Warm - Busy inspecting Sanitary Arrangements	Fine Warm
"	18	1 am	Had orders to be in readiness to report for orders -	Fine Warm
"	19	12 noon	2 Officers + 30 Mor-5 who returned from 28th Fld Amb, ready to move to prepare to move in	Fine Warm
"			Who at Full Strength.	Fine
"	22	10 am	DDMS 2nd Corps inspects unit.	Fine
"	26		Showers	
"	27	8.15 am	2 Officers + 58 other ranks proceeded to PONT d. NIEPPE on advance party on trains and bus	Showers
"		8.30 am	30 mor-5 proceed to NIEPPE for duty in same Square - This 7 men - remainder has been employed in drills + practical stretcher returning to Appendix 6.	
"			32 NCO's & men duly reported for General Duties with ADS — Additional equipment has been drawn Unit consist chiefly Stretchers - hand wheeled Stretchers, Sub units (on top Kitchen) extra dressings coffee blankets and Joint Equipment on not table forms - All kits has been collected - dressings parties have been issued (a2 Sittings prepared for the purpose & notes preparation in regard to the — Sorting of the Injury on establishment has been received. 1 Sect. 1 Wagon 1 Advance Park Amb. AFC (MT) - 1 Motor Lorry - 1 Driver ASC (MT) - Proceeded & LA CRECHE for 2 days from to bring out from 2nd Fld Amb.	

Russell –
Newhirst

1875 Wt. W593/826 1,000,000 4/15 J.B.C. & A. A.D.S.S./Forms/C. 2118.

July 1st 1916

DAG Base

Herewith War diary for
month of June for
140th Field Ambulance

R Wilmot
Major OC 140 F Amb

COMMITTEE FOR THE MEDICAL HISTORY OF THE WAR

Date 5 AUG. 1915

1407.aml.
Army Form C. 2118.
Vol 2
Feun

WAR DIARY
or
INTELLIGENCE SUMMARY
(Erase heading not required.)

Place	Date	Hour	Summary of Events and Information	Remarks and references to Appendices
LA CRECHE	June 1	2 pm	Moved to PONT DE NIEPPE and took over the driving Station Zone & A.D.S. Brewery	
PONT DE NIEPPE	" 3		PLOEGSTEERT - LE BIZET Road from 28th Field Ambulance. 4 pm	
"	" 4		36 wounded through driving Station during the evening - mostly from Reat 6 R.W.K.	
			G.O.C. 41st Div. inspected the driving Station - Inspected A.D.S. in afternoon - fine - windy	
	" 5		DDMS to Corps inspected main driving Station. Fine cloudy.	
	" 6		Rain. R.A.P. Hart attached to 21 KRR for temporary duty	
	" 7		Fine.	
	" 8		Inspected Motor Car Corner for a place for dump for wounded from No 6 R.A.P.	
	" 9		A.D.S. shelled 18" whizzbangs - Some slight damage to Equipment.	
	" 10	6 am 10-1	about 100-150 rounds - hit 15 direct hits. No Casualties. Rain	
	" 11	5 pm	Inspected ADS.	
	" 12		Rain. Very wet.	
	" 15		Still very cold wet - R.A.P. Hart attached to 21 KRR for permanent duty	
	" 16		Fine cold - Visited A.D.S.	
	" 17	12.50 am 2.50 am	Gas alarm. 3 no gas in Brewery Station of A.D.S. 1 Canary gassing installed to (Brewery Station) 1 drift 1 shell.	
			(Resumed normal Conditions)	
	" 18		Gas alarm.	
	" 19	11.45 pm 1.45 am	Resumed normal Conditions { No ammunition for far } We far in Brewery Station areas	
	" 21		Weather fine. Cold Since 18th. Wind Variable Southerly since 16th. Visits ADS - No 6 RAP	
	" 22	10.50 am	Pont du Niepp. bridge Shelled for about 40 minutes about a dozen 13" No Casualties.	
			amongst SOldin. 3 or 4 Slight Cases among women Civilians. Warm, fine.	
	" 23		Violent thunder storm 5 pm with heavy rain - Shells West end of Pont de Nieppe about 9 pm	
	" 24		Captain Hogg friend vice L. Hart	
			DDMS V Corps V ADMS 41 Div. in-fielded	
				Rov

Army Form C. 2118

WAR DIARY
or
INTELLIGENCE SUMMARY
(Erase heading not required.)

Instructions regarding War Diaries and Intelligence Summaries are contained in F.S. Regs., Part II. and the Staff Manual respectively. Title Pages will be prepared in manuscript.

Place	Date	Hour	Summary of Events and Information	Remarks and references to Appendices
Puits de Nieppe	June 27		Rain. ADMS informed me that we should probably have to move our headquarters shortly as we are in another division area. Inspected School 96 Rue D'Armentieres Nieppe for a billet. This is at present occupied by Intelligence Corps & Division.	
	28		Rain	
	29		Fine. Quiet	
	30		A more busy day 71 wounded admitted up till 8 a.m. July 1 from noon 30th June.	

R. Andrewes
Major DC 140 FAmb

W 188. S 324. (for 15 – 30 June 1916)
Daily W. av = 7.79. Daily sick 20.45

Scabies   = 61   = 18.8%
Dental   = 21   = 6.5%
Influenza = 21   = 6.5%
I.C.T   = 17   = 5.2%
Myalgia   = 15   = 4.6%
Bronchitis = 8   = 2.4%
Syph + gon = 7   = 2.1%
Impetigo   = 7   = 2.1%
Boils   = 5   = 1.5%
Diarrhœa   = 5   = 1.5%

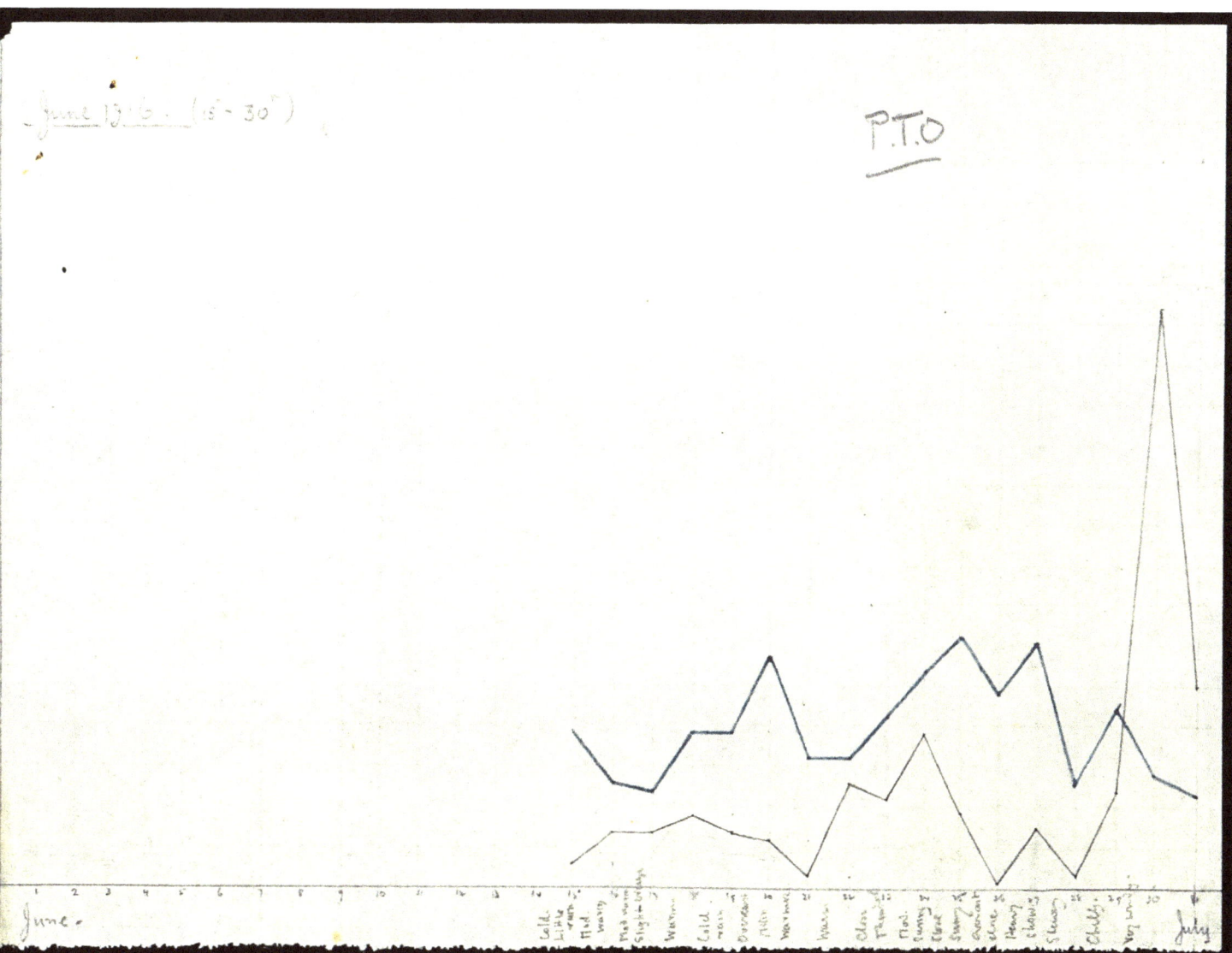

— July —

W = 350   S = 580.

Daily average = 11.2%

Sick = 16.7%

Scabies	= 143	=	22.9%
Influenza	= 35	=	6.03%
Dental	= 31	=	5.3%
Myalgia	= 30	=	5.2%
S.L.G	= 20	=	3.4%
Optical	= 20	=	3.4%
Mines Thorn	= 14	=	2.4%
Tonsilitis	= 18	=	3.2%
Soft Tissue	= 12	=	2.1%
Scabies	= 10	=	1.7%
Boils	= 10	=	1.7%
Mumps	= 10	=	1.7%
Bronchitis	= 8	=	1.4%
Syph + Gon.	= 7	=	1.2%
Sinusitis	= 7	=	1.2%
Ulcers	= 5	=	0.93%
Diarrhoea	= 5	=	0.85%
Syphilis	= 3	=	0.5%
Scarlet Fever	= 1	=	0.17%

4/— July Vol 3

Confidential
Fan Duty
Not been Published

To cost £3
July, 1916.

COMMITTEE FOR THE
MEDICAL HISTORY OF THE WA[R]
Date 5 – SEP 2[?]

ORIGINAL 140 Field Ambulance

WAR DIARY or **INTELLIGENCE SUMMARY**
(Erase heading not required.)

Army Form C. 2118

MEDICAL

Place	Date	Hour	Summary of Events and Information	Remarks and references to Appendices
Pont de Nieppe	July 2	2.30pm	Visited working parties in PLOEGSTEERT. Fine weather.	
	-5	3 pm	Visited A.D.S & Lawrence Farm after extension of the line this morning - Centre battalion now have two aid posts Lawrence Farm & Reserve Farm. The former has returned from the advanced dressing station MO & 1 man.	
	-9	11 am	GOC 41st Division inspected main & advanced dressing stations - all out. Satisfactory - The battery at JESENELLE fire across the road was being shelled all the morning. 6.15 PM 7 pm 4 pm & 5 pm. The Sergt Major of this battery was hit & to the Savile went to give surgical assistance whilst the battery was being shelled. He died after 2 hrs.	
	-10		Fine. Recd by 2nd KRR 12.44 1/B at night all casualties easily dealt with.	
	-13		Fine & cold last few nights. Rain at night.	
	-15	aft	NIEPPE shelled 2 officers admitted to main dressing station wounded from there. Lieut: Harrison left for temporary duty with 19th Middlesex during absence of MO sick. Lieut Bruford went to 32nd Royal Fusiliers in medical charge via KREUZ VERMA - transferred to Field Ambulance.	
	-16			
	-17		NIEPPE Shelled 1 man admitted wounded from there	
	-18		NIEPPE Shelled 1 Officer & 2 men admitted wounded from there	
	-19	2 pm	PONT de NIEPPE hotel shelled 15 civilians & 7 military casualties from there 6 were killed - brien Jakob in the main dressing station. no casualties 15 came with ambulance train to divisional Red X stat.	
	-20		ADMS inspected the main dressing station.	
	-24		Pte Moore Saddler became hit in shoulder & evacuated (first casualty in unit)	
	-25		To Motor Car Corner R.A.P. Survey Farm. 23rd Middlesex - Barrage of fire on was to to Motor Car Corner held up, Car brought them V then arrived through - weather dull for fine the past ten days.	

1875 Wt W593/826 1,000,000 4/15 J.B.C. & A. A.D.S.S./Forms/C. 2118.

ORIGINAL

140th Field Ambulance

WAR DIARY or INTELLIGENCE SUMMARY

Army Form C. 2118

MEDICAL

(Erase heading not required.)

Place	Date	Hour	Summary of Events and Information	Remarks and references to Appendices
PONT DE NIEPPE	July 26	11 pm	Artillery bombardment preceding front line	
		1 am	Raid by 10th (Queens) R. West Surrey & 20th Durham Light Infantry.	
		2 am	First casualties from 20th D.L.I.	
	27	7 am	100 casualties of (20th D.L.I & 10th Queens Chiefly) also a few of that unit had been evacuated to C.C.S. BAILLEUL. Medical arrangements were as follows :- Evacuation from R.A.P's :- 10th Queens - 8 Stretcher bearers with 4 Stretchers & blankets at aid post for evacuation to Advanced Dressing Station - Supplied by the Field Ambulance for evacuation to M.D.S. 20th D.L.I. 8 Stretcher bearers similar at aid post for evacuation to loading ambulance Car Used - Terminus trolley line - Where 1 Corpl & 1 man were posted for loading ambulance cars - In each car evacuation was by trolley line. Cars - At M.D.S. - 5/4 & Motor cars carried to main dressing Station by Motor Ambulances from Adv. Dr. Stn. & fro Service - Two cars were employed for each spot & kept up a continuous service - Arrangement at main Dressing Station. for unloading Field Ambulance cars carried to Receiving room & loading C.C.S. cars N.C.O. & 3 men were employed:- a Supply of Stretchers & Blankets were kept at the Entrance for replenishing Field Amb. Cars under the above N.C.O. This N.C.O. was responsible for obtaining nominal rolls from the office of men for C.C.S. car & seeing the cars were loaded according to this role - the role going to C.C.S. with the cases. Cases were disposed by the unloading party in 2 Groups (i) Serious (ii) Slight in the space of the Dressing Station.	

WAR DIARY or INTELLIGENCE SUMMARY

Army Form C. 2118

140th Field Ambulance — MEDICAL

Place	Date	Hour	Summary of Events and Information	Remarks and references to Appendices
PONT à NIEPPE	July 27		Receiving & Dressing of Cases:- Two Officers Capt Rowbotham & Lieut Harrison each had charge of a Receiving & Dressing Room - They had for staff each 1 NCO for Dispenser & ambulance Serum Clerk & 4 dressers. The former took the Serious Cases and the latter the Sitting Cases - Serious Cases were collected into 2 areas (a) lying (b) sitting - These were fed by the help of the Chaplains in priority to carry lieu & onto stretchers. The forms was prepared by two Clerks. A Senior NCO was in charge of the Patients & was responsible for counting the Blankets on the Stretchers & for making them up into car loads; giving the Serial number of each case to the three accompanying Car loads - This NCO was also responsible for checking the Stretchers & Blankets taken from the C.C.S. Cars in exchange - These being out being in excess of those received. One Clerk at Entrance gave each case on arrival a blank Medical Card with Serial number for A.D. book attached & Kept record of the numbers in a book. Serial number for separate Serial numbers to the men. There were from separate Serial numbers including Serial The Clerks in the receiving rooms filled in slips with all particulars including Serial Number for A.D. Book for each case. The Medical Cards were also filled in by these Clerks. The Cases were then known by their Serial number for purpose of evacuation. Two Clerks in the Office prepared nominal rolls (with full particulars) of car loads from the Serial Numbers as given by the Senior NCO in filled in the A.D. Book.	

ORIGINAL

Army Form C. 2118

WAR DIARY
or
INTELLIGENCE SUMMARY   MEDICAL
(Erase heading not required.)

140th Field Ambulance

Place	Date	Hour	Summary of Events and Information	Remarks and references to Appendices
PONT DE NIEPPE	July 27		PACK STRS 1 NCO & 1 man were employed in Pack Store & received all iron helmets and arms & ammunition & equipment from — No men had packs. With then two officers one NCO /& 2 NCOs (chauffeurs) 8 drivers, 5 clerks scouts & feeding 2 sanitors 1 NCO & 6 men for loading & unloading 100 patients were dressed in the field Ambulance & evacuated to CCS within 5 hours and there were several stark intervals of no work and 1 hour when no cases were brought in for dressing & the personnel had their breakfast. All ranks of ADS & MDS worked exceedingly well — and the MO W. Queens were especially thanking L/Cpl Williams for his assistance at his Aid Post. 13 Owen horse through the last few carts coming in at long intervals in our care 24 hours after — Weather hot & fine — damp mist in each morn —	
	28	11.15p	NIEPPE shelled & heavy artillery 5.9 & 8in 9 inch 3 killed & 14 wounded military. Owing damage to the church. Gas alarm 1am 29th No attack	
	31		Weather has been dry & hot for past few days on a famous full today very hot. The total number of admissions to hospital in June & July.	Appendix attached

	Sick.	Wounded.	S & C.	Wounded
June		July		
Officers	16	15	30	19
O Ranks	615	277	550	331

31 NIEPPE shelled for 1 hour — 1 casualty a child age 2 yr —

R.C. Mulvik
Major 7 Comm
OC 140 F Amb

MEDICAL

Army Form C. 2118

140th Field Ambulance

WAR DIARY
or
INTELLIGENCE SUMMARY
(Erase heading not required.)

Instructions regarding War Diaries and Intelligence Summaries are contained in F.S. Regs., Part II. and the Staff Manual respectively. Title Pages will be prepared in manuscript.

Place	Date	Hour	Summary of Events and Information	Remarks and references to Appendices
PONT DE NIEPPE	August 5		Very quiet past 5 days. Weather fine. Pont de Nieppe Shelled shrapnel about 8 bursts above church. No casualties.	
		3 pm		
	6	4.30 pm	NIEPPE Shelled. 3 casualties. Fine.	
	7	9.35 am	PONT DE NIEPPE shelled 2 wounds shrapnel 3 high explosive near X roads N of church 3 casualties (1 soldier 1 civilian man 1 child) Weather fine	
		3.30 pm	NIEPPE Shelled	
	9	11.10 am	Message from left reserve 123 1BSC for ambulance cars Lieut. DAVIES - Shelling at road junction PONT DE NIEPPE	
		11.20	2 cars left for LE BIZET (left reserve 123 1 Bde)	
		11.40	LE BIZET - PLOEGSTEERT. 2s wounded 115 Queens all evacuated (dressed) to CCS.	
		12.45	1 Shell high explosive into PONT DE NIEPPE X roads no casualty	
		12.50 pm	NIEPPE Shelled 1 casualty - Fine + hot past few days.	
	13		Weather fine + hot. Sure last entry - very quiet.	
		8.30 pm	Received orders for Field Ambulance to be ready to move out of PONT DE NIEPPE to new area. V Corps.	
	14		Hot showery. ADMS 23rd Div with ADMS 4th Div inspected Dressing Station + Advanced Dressing Station.	
	15		Rain Showery system	
	16	3.30 pm	Advanced party 69 FA arrived	
	17	7 pm	OC 69 Fd Amber came to inspect Dressing Station + Advanced Dressing Station. Showed him round + Pooled Dugouts	
	18	6.15 am	handed over	
		6.30 am	parade to move out	
			Marched out	
METEREN	19	9.35 am	Arrived fine	
	20		Rain. Route March	
	21		Stann in morning. Field Ambulance Sports in afternoon.	
			ROUTE MARCH	

MEDICAL
140th Field Ambulance

Army Form C. 2118

WAR DIARY
or
INTELLIGENCE SUMMARY
(Erase heading not required.)

Place	Date	Hour	Summary of Events and Information	Remarks and references to Appendices
METEREN	August 22	11 pm	Packed baggage. Fine. Marched out to entrain at BAILLEUL WEST station.	
BAILLEUL WEST Station.	23	12.15 am	Started entrainment with 299 Coy ASC. Side loading.	
		2 am	Entrainment completed for 140 Field Ambulance & 299 Coy ASC	
		2.10 am	A mule hung in its chain in the truck & died.	
		2.50 am	Mules unloaded in this truck & retrucked	
		3.28 am	Train left practically to time.	
PONT REMY		12.25 pm	Train arrived 1hr 20 min late.	
		2.15 pm	Train unloaded & all horses & vehicles clear of station after difficult side unloading with ramps to the front and different side unloading with ramps to the front	
EAUCOURT		3 pm	Arrived in billets & started cleaning up.	
	24	6.30 am to 6.30 pm	Training parties in field ambulance exercises. Fine. Showery. Visited 1.4 1.Bde at 3.30 pm.	
	25		Training as yesterday. 2 Sections did exercise with one Section patients.	
		11 am	Visited Divisional headquarters. Showery in morning after a fine day.	
	26	6.30-7.30 am	Squad drill physical exercises & bathing	
		9-5 pm	Field day.	
		8.30-10.30 pm	Route march orderlies detailed en route to carry messages to a definite point. Rain.	
	29	5 am	A combined Divisional exercise carried out for 3 field ambulances. Marched out of billets to starting point for exercise 7 miles away, had breakfast en route & arrived 1 mile beyond AILLY at 9 am where 1st division lines "Beecher" filled a dressing station. Beam division collected wounded with other 2 ambulances - all pioneer battalion as wounded - DDMS × Corps & ADMS×8Div inspected the exercise	

WAR DIARY or INTELLIGENCE SUMMARY
(Erase heading not required.)

Army Form C. 2118

MEDICAL
140th Field Ambulance

Place	Date	Hour	Summary of Events and Information	Remarks and references to Appendices
EAUCOURT	Aug 29	4 pm	Exercise finished arrived back at billets. A heavy thunderstorm from 2=30 - 6 pm -	
		7.30pm	Rain daily since 24th inst until today which has been fine.	
	31		Training for the Field Ambulance has been carried out as programme attached	3.
			Chart of Sick recommended for more thorough attention attached	4.

Appendix D.

Programme of Training for One Week, commencing Saturday August 26th 1916

Day	6.30 – 7.30	9 – 1	2 – 5	5.30 – 6.30	Evening.
Saturday Aug 26	A Sect } Squad Drill. B " } C " } Phys. Drill.	Field Day		Nil.	Route March
Sunday Aug 27	Nil.	Church Services, Bathing Parade, Washing Clothes			
Monday Aug 28	A Sect } Phys. Drill B " } Stretcher Drill with patients C " }	Work in conjunction with infantry battalion. Section of a Field Ambulance a battalion		Officers. Writing reports orders + messages. Men. Practical instr in bandaging.	
Tuesday Aug 29	Route March with Transport – 12 miles. 1 hours halt for breakfast.				Collecting wounded 1½ hours.
Wednesday Aug 30	A Sect } Str. drill C " } with patients B " } Phys. Drill	Stretcher drill with prepared stretchers. Collecting wounded – Position of patients with regard to injury.	Tent Pitching	Officers. Interior economy of a Fd Amb. Men. Squad Drill.	
Thursday Aug 31	A Sect } Str. drill with patients B " } C " } Phys. Drill	Field Day. All N.C.O's above rank of Corporal to be patients. Lower ranks will take their places for the various duties.		Nil.	
Friday Sept 1.	Loading Motor Ambulance Wagons.	Route March by Sections without transport. Messages to be sent by foot orderly to Head Quarters.	2-3 Lectures on haemorrhage + shock + their treatment. 3-5 Making of Latrines, incinerators + urine tubs.	Nil.	Route March.

Appendix 4.

Aug		W		S				
1		W	1	S	30	Scabies	= 67	= 17.3%
2		W	1	S	19	Influenza	= 34	= 8.8%
3		W	3	S	16	V.D.G.	= 22	= 5.6
4		W	3	S	13			
5		W	1	S	13	Myalgia	= 18	= 4.6%
6		W	4	S	4	Dental	= 17	= 4.4%
7		W	4	S	10	Boils	= 15	= 3.8%
8		W	1	S	25	Debility	= 11	= 2.8%
9		W	26	S	9	Hernia	= 12	= 3.0%
10		W	2	S	10	Diarrhoea	= 7	= 1.8%
11		W	2	S	5	Lymph + Gon:	= 6	= 1.5%
12		W	0	S	19	Neurasthenia	= 5	= 1.3%
13		W	0	S	16	Tonsilitis	= 5	= 1.3%
14		W	5	S	20	Enteritis	= 5	= 1.3%
15		W	1	S	23	Appendicitis	= 5	= 1.3%
16		W	1	S	12	I.D.S.	= 5	= 1.3%
17				S	9	Infl. of Scrotum	= 3	= .75%
18				S	9	Abcess	= 3	= .75%
19				S	6	Bronchitis	= 3	= .75%
20				S	9	Obstical	= 2	= .5%
21				S	12	Scarlet Fever	= 1	= .25%
22				S	8	Measles	= 1	= .25%
23				S	0	Cerebro Spinal Mening.	= 1	= .25%
24				S	7			
25				S	15			
26				S	13			
27				S	6			
28				S	15			
29				S	14			
30				S	11			
31				S	10			

Total Wounded = 55   Average daily total of Wounded = 3.2 (Aug 1-16 whilst in line)
Total Sick = 387   "   "   "   " Sick   = 12.5 for whole month

August

140/18/15

War Diary
of
110th Field Amb

1st Quarter

from

1st October to 30th December
1916

(VOLUME V)

Oct. 1916

VOLS

COMMITTEE FOR THE
MEDICAL HISTORY OF THE WAR
Date -9 DEC. 1916

VOLUME V

140 Field Ambulance Army Form C. 2118

MEDICAL

WAR DIARY
or
INTELLIGENCE SUMMARY
(Erase heading not required.)

Instructions regarding War Diaries and Intelligence Summaries are contained in F.S. Regs., Part II. and the Staff Manual respectively. Title Pages will be prepared in manuscript.

Place	Date	Hour	Summary of Events and Information	Remarks and references to Appendices
EAUCOURT	Sept 1	9-5 8:30-10	Training as per schedule. 2 cases of suspected Cerebro-Spinal Meningitis in 183 Bde RFA 33 Generals evacuated to hosp. at EAUCOURT. Bathing in which the cases remained up for the line.	
			Fought Rev Fine	
			Personal	
	2		Training as per schedule. Afternoon taken up in serving out equipment & medical equipment. Fine. Rev	
	3		Bathing parade 8:30 am – Reconnaissance of ground for divisional medical exercise ERGNIES, BROCAMPS district	
		10.30 am	Horse Show. Rain in afternoon. 140 F Amb 1½s. in jumping no reply from	
		3 pm 3.30 pm 5 pm	Brown division moved out to bivouac ready for divisional exercise – bivouacs in E of AILLY & HAUTCLOCHEU Rev Rest division line 'B' Sector moved out for divisional medical exercise	
	4	7 am		
		11 am	orders to return home owing to orders for a move	
		2 pm	Rest division arrives at billets	
		3.30 pm	Brown division arrived at billets	
			Cerebro Spinal Suspected cases found negative – contacts returned to duty by Major Bowtwood	
	5		R.A. headquarters at DERNANCOURT. Drawing Station MONFLIERS closed 8 p.m. Orders received for Regiment to move under command of Captain HOGG left to proceed by ROUTE MARCH Transport line B motor ambulances to	
		1.10 am 1.30 pm	with Brigade Group transport for XV Corps area. Fine Showery Rev	
	6	8.30 am	Lieut LACEY proceeded to LONGPRÉ station to report to 122 Brigade headquarters for billeting officers for the 140 Field Ambulance. Fine Rev	
	7	7.30 am 8 am	Reveille Paraded & marched out	

Army Form C. 2118

WAR DIARY
or
INTELLIGENCE SUMMARY
(Erase heading not required.)

140 Field Ambulance
MEDICAL

Place	Date	Hour	Summary of Events and Information	Remarks and references to Appendices
LONGRÉ les Corps Ecurie	Sept 7	7.18 am 8.50 am 9 am 11.30 am 3.30 pm	arrived Railway Station. Motor ambulances left for MERICOURT Station by road. Entrained. Motor ambulances arrived MERICOURT Station arrived Station. Personnel.	
MERICOURT	—	6.45 pm 8.20 pm	personnel arrived. Transport arrived. Fine - cold - windy. Rcw	
Camp E9 6.2.D. N. Albert	— 8		In camp Nil Rcw C Section lut Subdivision under command Captain Davidson left for Corps Main Dressing Station also MASH left for temporary duty with 5th Middlesex BECORDEL	
	— 9	3.30 pm	Moved to Camp BECORDEL 2 miles in the S.W. Fine.	
Camp N° BECORDEL	— 9	5.20 pm 6 pm	arrived in camp. Rcw Fine Camp pitched - Tea.	app 4
	— 10	12 noon 3 pm	Packed up & parked wagons for men left for BELLE VUE Farm E ʃ ALBERT	
BELLE VUE Farm ALBERT		3.20 pm 6 pm	arrived Horsed Ambulance wagons left for Divisional Collecting Station for walking wounded 2 - Fine also Motor Ambulance Cars No 2 - Rcw	
	— 11	2 pm 9 am	Lieut Davies left for duty with Heavy Artillery Group as M.O. Bearer division under command of Captain Hogg left for divisional collecting Station for walking wounded took over work with the 2 other field ambulances of the Division.	app 5
	"	12 pm 10 pm	took over Divisional Main dressing Station at BELLEVUE Farm from 1/3 West Lancs Field Ambulance Captain Rowbotham left for duty at Divisional Collecting Station thus leaving me the sole officer at the Headquarters of the Field Ambulance with (1) here but subdivisions personnel and (2) horse transport less Ambulance wagons & (3) 2 Motor Ambulance wagons. Rcw	

WAR DIARY or INTELLIGENCE SUMMARY

Army Form C. 2118

140th Field Ambulance
MEDICAL

Place	Date	Hour	Summary of Events and Information	Remarks and references to Appendices
BELLEVUE FME	Sept 12		Busy day alone at Divisional Main dressing station – 445 Sick in day – Evacuated to 64 Corps Rest Station 14 Casualty Clearing Station – 5 Divisional Sick were seen – 11 cases of Diarrhoea and Intestinal complaints – Fine weather. Improvements to Camp as per schedule.	
	– 13		Usual day in morning, seeing sick & found the Club 40 remaining.	
		2 pm	To Advanced dressing station Quarry N of MONTAUBAN and to see the Green Dump North of this and West of LONGUEVAL. Had two interviews with ADMS on pending operations. Edw & fins	Rev
	– 14	12 noon	Captain ROWBOTHAM returned for duty at Headquarters – Handed over patients in the Dressing Station to Captain ROWBOTHAM. Have two interviews with ADMS over the pending operations after supper.	
		9.00 am 9.00am	Received operation order No 1 ADMS saying to be in position at GREEN DUMP at 11 pm. – Remainder of equipment to be there under Major Williamson O.C. 136 Field Ambulance arrangements –	
		5.30 p	Left to take up position at GREEN DUMP.	
GREEN DUMP SW of LONGUEVAL		8.30 pm	Arrived at GREEN DUMP having called at 136 Headquarters on MARICZ – MONTAUBAN road & sent & found the bearer division of 140 Field Ambulance were still there & the GREEN DUMP skeleton away – what in reality in advance to Sunken Road ground. At the GREEN DUMP found Captain HOGG had (dug out which was very just finished) into the bivouac & material which had had sent up previously from BAZENTINE – There was a shortage of sticks & pillows for stretchers & of stretchers generally. These were asked for from the ADS at the Quarry	Rev
	15	5.00 am	It was found that 138 Bearer Division who were at the Regimental Aid Post were not as numerous as expected & the relief of these bearers had been or through the dugouts not being relieved until 3 am. Public C. W. 140 Field Bearer Division 2 am 7.00 a.m. Brancer had taken place at 8 KRR Battalion.	

WAR DIARY or INTELLIGENCE SUMMARY

Army Form C. 2118

140th Field Ambulance
MEDICAL

Place	Date	Hour	Summary of Events and Information	Remarks and references to Appendices
GREEN DUMP	15 Sept		a Sergeant to proceed forthwith with one of the 138th F.Amb bearers as a guide. There will now 20 bearers of 140th Field Ambulance with a NCO with each party at each of the Regimental aid posts in the line.	
		6.30am	Capt HOGG with 40 bearers, 20 for each aid post. A NCO for each party left to reinforce the aid posts. Two hours had not been communicated to me in writing but was informed at 6.30am (1½ hours at which operations were to commence). This left 88 men at the GREEN DUMP for discharging cases & for reinforcements for bearers. 138th F.Amb bearer subdivision being Veryweak & consisting of 1 NCO & 18 men only — Wounded had been brought in a steady stream during the night & had been easily coped with.	
		8.30am	Wounded were now coming in in large numbers chiefly from the New Zealand division and in resistance being demanded from MO 1st Bn 3rd N Zealand R.B. I sent 8 men with 4 stretchers	
		9.30am	to obtain resistance through his own A.D.M.S. as I was unable to cope with his division informed the MO to 41st Div. left sector (122 Inf Reg) for whom I was responsible.	
		11 am	Wounded were now beginning to accumulate at GREEN DUMP. I personally, in addition to all available personnel at the DUMP was busily employed in dressing cases & made several appeals for cars to get forward to remove wounded. I then obtained assistance of every vehicle which came to the dump & also of German prisoners which were now beginning to come in, as bearers to evacuate wounded to the ADS at the Quarry. As so many of these cases had come to the DUMP without being dressed, a large amount of work had to be done to dress these cases & prepare them for transport.	
		12 noon	Evacuation was going on with difficulty from the line but satisfactorily, and the DUMP was now getting well cleared & after this we had no block there.	
		5.30pm	Captain HOGG returned & reported that numerous cases had been dressed & were ready for evacuation	

WAR DIARY
or
INTELLIGENCE SUMMARY

(Erase heading not required.)

Army Form C. 2118

110th Field Ambulance
MEDICAL

Instructions regarding War Diaries and Intelligence Summaries are contained in F.S. Regs., Part II. and the Staff Manual respectively. Title Pages will be prepared in manuscript.

Place	Date	Hour	Summary of Events and Information	Remarks and references to Appendices
	16.	7 am	The Bearer Section were becoming exhausted. These were pulled out at 2.30pm they were sent out under command of Captain W.A. HARRISON who had moved from B. A.D.S. The GREEN DUMP had now been successfully cleared and all cases were being moved directly to the A.D.S. by 2nd Australian Casualty Station wheels, German prisoners & vehicles which were returning empty of all descriptions. R.O.W. Wounded from the line & clearing of the GREEN DUMP Head on successfully during the night. No hand and ten able to keep up the movement forward through the Dump but it is estimated that fully 2000 wounded passed through in the first 24 hours. These casualties were from 6th & 8th Divisions. New Second Div, 17th Div, 21st Div, 24th Div. Besides a few men of other Divisions.	
		10 am	48 men of that division A.V.B. Sections 110th Field Ambulance arrived for assistance & information was received that Argus FONSUTHAM & Laigney men to bearer were retained later. Were to return to Advanced that Argus FONSUTHAM - MONTAUBAN road at 12 noon & Capt ROBERTSON & OR was command a dump on MAMETZ - MONTAUBAN road. Medical at the dump Captain HOBB had left the 50th Regt 30 M.O. & 32 Bearers were Medical at the dump. Lieut LACEY & two men was sent to 11 R.West Kents from 8 Gordon Williams command. No car ran accidents. Lieut LACEY & two men was sent to 11 R.West Kents from 8 Gordon Williams command.	
		11.30 am	8 men of the that division were detailed at the Dump that remained as dressers, Speed & 5 Also the dumps & 40 infantry men who had been employed formed to section under a Sergeant & R.E. as a guide & reinforce were distributed, stretchered to the line under a Sergeant & R.E. as a guide & reinforce Captain HARRISON's Post.	
		3.20pm	Remained here at camp on MAMETZ - MONTAUBAN road & had a meal, all food sauce In tins refrigerated & a Stew.	
		7 pm	Received orders to proceed to the CRUCIFIX on LONGUEVAL - MONTAUBAN road & from an A.D.S. Motor transport that Captain ROWBOTHAM and other men had & Personnel necessary were sent (One Officer was ordered from DUBOY Wood under a N.O. ack to Junction)	

1875   Wt. W593/826   1,000,000   4/15   J.B.C. & A.   A.D.S.S./Forms/C. 2118.

140th Field Ambulance

MEDICAL

Army Form C. 2118

WAR DIARY
or
INTELLIGENCE SUMMARY
(Erase heading not required.)

Place	Date	Hour	Summary of Events and Information	Remarks and references to Appendices
CRUCIFIX SQ LONGUEVAL	16-	8.30 pm	2 Officers & 2 bearer subdivisions 21st Div 170 Stretcher bearers R.W. Kents Bearer Division 139 F Amb. 1 Bearer Subdivision 138 F Amb. On arrival at CRUCIFIX at 8.30 pm I found Captain ROWBOTHAM had not arrived & Captain LAUDER 138 F Amb from whom he was to have taken over had left. The 2 bearer Sub-divisions 21 Div were weak in numbers No Stretcher bearers of R.W. Kents were available. There were 48 lying cases here for evacuation. These were rapidly evacuated to the Divisional Collecting station by divisional cars which were here in plenty & Horse Ambulances as far as	
		9.15 pm 9.45 pm	????? ????? ???? ????? ???? ????? ???? ???? ????? ???? I proceeded with Major WILLIAMSON to A.D.S. Quarry just about bearers of 140 Fd Ambce & what had (This party of bearers were collected) arrived at CROSS ROADS between ????? CROSSROADS Turning to Captain LAUDER ???? ????? I ordered the 1 WO & 6 S↓ remaining of the unit at headquarters to bring the necessary equipment (detailed) to form an A.D.S. at the SHRINE.	
		11.10	took over at the SHRINE after seeing MAJOR WILLIAMSON O.C. 138 F Amb ce & who was apparently conducting operations as regards evacuation of the line generally (viz O.C. 2 A Amb) I then found personnel as under 2 Off & 64 O.Ranks 21 DW 10 " 34 " 140 F Amb (This was Cpt ROWBOTHAM & party who arrived shortly 139 " after my arrival) 138 "	Rw

40th Field Ambulance

MEDICAL

WAR DIARY or INTELLIGENCE SUMMARY

Army Form C. 2118

(Erase heading not required.)

Place	Date	Hour	Summary of Events and Information	Remarks and references to Appendices
CRUCIFIX or SHRINE	17th	Midnight	Messages received that bearers were needed at BROWN & GREEN trenches	
		12.25 am 1.15 am 1.15 am	N.C.O. & men left for above trenches having procured a man as a guide. Message received OC. 136 7A from Lt ROCHE that a dump was formed on LONGUEVAL-FLERS R'd in S of FLERS. Lt POOLE with 1 Sgt & 39 men & 3 Ford Cars were sent with a guide to clear from in front of LONGUEVAL Wood & from dump formed by Lieut ROCHE.	
		3.35 am	A runner coming with a patient gave information of 2 off. & 30 O. Ranks wounded collected N.E. of DELVILLE Wood - Capt MENZIES & 24 bearers were sent to carry to the road where Ford Cars could then back to A.D.S.	
		7.30 am	12 men with 18-stretchers & 2 stretcher wheels were sent to assist in evacuation & report having been received that cars could not proceed for along the road by day owing to enemy shell fire - a dump was now formed at SW corner of DELVILLE Wood.	
		8.55 am	Having received a message from ADMS that the 140 Field Ambulance was to move to the SHRINE, I instructed Major WILLIAMSON to forward the personnel & equipment at the SHRINE. Lieut SH ADM'S verbal orders meant the SHRINE. Major Williamson was now in command at the SHRINE having proceeded from Sergt SIDDONS & some of 140 F. Amb. ce personnel arrived at the SHRINE	
		12 noon	The GREEN DUMP to FLERS to collect wounded, with orders to return with wounded to the SHRINE, at about the same time Corp. ANNAND & 28 men 140 F. Amb. arrived from the QUARRY. Just before the arrival of these parties I proceeded through DELVILLE WOOD with a view to seeing where Cars could proceed & where a dump for wounded could be formed. I met Captain LAUDER in the wood & we chose a spot on the left of the FLERS road at the N. western outskirts of the wood. Wounded to be cleared by hand & stretcher carriage to this spot.	

140th Field Ambulance

WAR DIARY or INTELLIGENCE SUMMARY
Army Form C. 2118 — MEDICAL
(Erase heading not required.)

Place	Date	Hour	Summary of Events and Information	Remarks and references to Appendices
CRUCIFIX	17th	12 noon	Evacuation was going on satisfactorily + the patients were evacuated from the A.D.S. SHRINE with regularity. Owing to BARRAGE of fire evacuation from the line to A.D.S. was difficult but was being carried out regularly + drivers were in turn required to rest at the A.D.S. By now the personnel of 21st Div. had been relieved though I was unaware of this until I found none present. at about 8am two operating tents were erected for dressing wounds for the wounded but an officer in each - 2 new officers having reported for duty during the early hours of the morning. The A.D.M.S. had inspected at about 7.30am + given orders for Major WILLIAMSON to be in charge of the A.D.S. Crucifix + I was to carry on there until his orders. A message was received about midday that the division was to be relieved this night by 55th Division. Orders to Transport lines were sent to pack up remainder of equipment + be prepared to move at short notice.	
		6 pm	Evacuation has been going on regularly - The A.D.S. was shelled during the afternoon but no casualties incurred - Two men were hit in the early morning in the camp from a 'Trench mortar' from our own guns one Killed + one wounded.	
		11.30 pm	An advanced party from 55th Div came in - These were taken up the line to the Regd Aid posts + shown the position of the DUMP + the mode of evacuation explained.	
	18th	3.30 am	A further party of 20 men having arrived of 55th Div. They were sent to the DUMP to relieve the 140th Div men there.	
		6 am	Relief completed as regards 140 3rd Amb. - Some personnel of 139 Famb remained + 140. 3 Amb moved out.	
		12.15 pm	arrived at Camp E ALBERT. Heavy rain all day.	

WAR DIARY
or
INTELLIGENCE SUMMARY

(Erase heading not required.)

Army Form C. 2118

1/40th Field Ambulance
MEDICAL

Instructions regarding War Diaries and Intelligence Summaries are contained in F. S. Regs., Part II. and the Staff Manual respectively. Title Pages will be prepared in manuscript.

Place	Date	Hour	Summary of Events and Information	Remarks and references to Appendices
Camp E ALBERT Sheet 62D E15 a76	Sept 18.	12.30 pm	Put up bivouacs & prepared cookhouses, latrines, incinerators etc. Arranged for a fire ration for the Brigade.	
		10pm	Lieut FOLEY left for temporary duty at 36 CCS. RCM	
	19		Day spent in improving camp & checking equipment - about 12 men in the Brigadier. The Field Ambulance took dinners. Another wet day. RCM	
	20		Continued checking equipment & found several deficiencies in various items of equipment due no doubt to the number of moves & different commands in which this Revd. in the few days. Another wet day. Troops uncomfortable. RCM	
	21		A fine day - Inspected & cleaning medical & transport equipment to be made fit to move. ?? NCO's battalion Capt HOGG & 2nd O. Tavedo ??? of HENRY & Camp Auxiliar who so acts for withdrawn from NCO's immediately. 36 CCS raids ADMS orders -	
	22	5pm	2 NCO's 12 men for batts. VIVIER MILL VINCO & Larm & 10th HELLY Reg. Lieut DYSON & Lieut GANM reported for duty. RCM	
		6pm	A fine day - Cold. Equipment 2 NCO's & 7 men by Roe temp 1664	
	23		2 NCO's & 7 men returned from VIVIER MILL Rattn. Arranged for all men of the unit to get baths at VIVIER MILL BATHS. RCM Sun. Nothing until ? NCO's & battalions 124 & 122 3rd Reg. RCM	

1875 Wt. W593/826 1,000,000 4/15 J.B.C. & A. A.D.S.S./Forms/C. 2118.

WAR DIARY or INTELLIGENCE SUMMARY

(Erase heading not required.)

War diary
MEDICAL
140 Field Ambulance

Army Form C. 2118

Place	Date	Hour	Summary of Events and Information	Remarks and references to Appendices
Camp E ALBERT	Sept 24	11 am	Lieut DYSON & Lieut GAMM to 36 C.C.S. Vice Captain E.S. ROWBOTHAM & Captain ROWBOTHAM returned to Field Ambulance – Fine Rev	
	24	10 pm	Raw	
	25		Orders received to stand to ready to move at 2 hours notice from 12.35 pm to support XV Corps – Fine Raw	
	26		A.D.M.S. inspected camp – Disinfector 244 Inf A.R lines preparatory programme. Fine hot Fine – Cooler. Raw	
	27		Rain Showery later Raw	
	28		Raw	
	29		Hot. There has been a considerable amount of sickness since returned from the line on 18th inst amongst the units of the two brigades 22" & 24" evacuating through this Field Ambulance – over 40 cases have been admitted during this period 119 of which have been Sent on to C.R.S. or C.C.S. Raw	
	30		Fine – Still in Camp Raw Chart attached marked app. 6	6.

R.C. Kienert
Major O.C. 140 Field Ambulance

app 4.

app 5

140th Field Ambulance Operation Order No 6 copy 2

Reference Map France Sh. 62D /40...

1. The bearer division under the command of Capt Hogg RAMC will move to D.C.S (Walking Wounded) at BECORDEL tomorrow (E7 b29)
2. No equipment except personal equipment will be carried
3. The unexpired portion of the days ration will be carried
4. Parade at 8.15
5. They will report on arrival to O.C D.C.S (W.W)
6. They will arrive at 9:0 am. approx distance 1½ miles.
7. Hour of arrival to be reported to this office.

Issued to
Copy No 1 File
         + War Diary
         + ...
         + ...
                                    R. ...
                                    Major KAME
                            Commanding 140th Field Ambulance

September

app. 6

1	S	17	Diarrhoea	= 60	=	20%
2	S	6	Influenza	= 42	=	14%
3	S	2	I.C.T	= 31	=	10.3%
4	S	4	Myalgia	= 19	=	6.3%
5	S	1	Scabies and Impetyo	= 15	=	5.0%
6	S	2	Sprains	= 12	=	4.0%
7	S	4	Boils	= 10	=	3.3%
8	S	8	Enteritis	= 10	=	3.3%
9	S	7	Dental	= 9	=	3.0%
10	S	8	Tonsilitis	= 5	=	1.6%
11	S	10	Inflam. Stomach	= 4	=	1.3%
12	S	29	Abcess	= 4	=	1.3%
13	S	15	Hernia	= 4	=	1.3%
14	S	16	Syph : Gon:	= 3	=	1.0%
15	S	12	Debility	= 3	=	1.0%
16	S	1	Bronchitis	= 2	=	.6%
17	S	0	Optical	= 1	=	.3%
18	S	0	Neurasthenia	= 1	=	.3%
19	S	2				
20	S	11				
21	S	17				
22	S	20				
23	S	17				
24	S	3				
25	S	12				
26	S	14				
27	S	13				
28	S	14				
29	S	17				
30	S	7				

Total Wounded = Nil
" Sick = 300
Daily Average = 10

Temperature ———
Sick ·········

SECRET

140/815

Vol 1

DUPLICATE
MEDICAL
War Diary

140th Field Amb.

41st Div.

COMMITTEE FOR THE
MEDICAL HISTORY OF THE WAR
Date -9 DEC. 1916

SHEET 1
Army Form C. 2118
Vol. VI

WAR DIARY
or
INTELLIGENCE SUMMARY
(Erase heading not required.)

Instructions regarding War Diaries and Intelligence Summaries are contained in F.S. Regs., Part II. and the Staff Manual respectively. Title Pages will be prepared in manuscript.

Place	Date	Hour	Summary of Events and Information	Remarks and references to Appendices
Camp E Albert	Oct 1	11 am	Totally fine day. Clocks went back 1hr at 1am to normal time - Church parade.	
	2		Rain 1 to 10 hours to Camp at X30 near MAMETZ. Row	
	3		Fine, showers later. Hut to accommodate for Camp at MAMETZ - BAZENTIN road in X29d. and W in touch with OC 139 (O/C evacuation) at FLAT IRON COPSE. Fds Ambulance in ANC but subdivision + 10 men of bearer division (at CCS + balls WEILLY) moved to camp at X29 d 4.5	
Camp at X29 d.4.5 MAMETZ - BAZENTIN Road		4.10 pm	Field Ambulance arrived at Camp. with 3 Officers + 15 O ranks arrived at camp X29	
		7 pm	Lieut DAVIES and 75 men and 1 horse ambulance wagon sent ahead proceeded to FLAT IRON COPSE to report to OC evacuation for bearer duties. Row	
	4	3.30 am	"B" Sector but subdivision w/commend of Captain ROWBOTHAM with Captain HOGG proceeded to GREENDUMP to take over ADS from N Zealand Field Ambulance -	
		10 am	Two horse ambulance wagons with water overalls proceeded to FLAT IRON COPSE for duty up the line, leaving 29 O. Ranks here -	
		4.15 pm	Capt Mc CRIRICK appointed for duty at FLAT IRON COPSE. Capt Mc CRIRICK proceeded to flat iron Copse	
	5		1 officer + 14 O ranks admitted to hospital sickly + detained reinforcement tins etc	

WAR DIARY or INTELLIGENCE SUMMARY

Army Form C. 2118

Place	Date	Hour	Summary of Events and Information	Remarks and references to Appendices
Camp X29.	Oct 5		Fine. Showery later.	
		9 am	Captain BINNIE & No 5 O. Ranks beaux division 138th Field Ambulance arrived for duty. Tent POCHÉ	
		7 pm	1 Sgt. + 30 O. Ranks 124 Inf. Bde. to FLAT IRON COPSE for beaux duties.	
		7.45 pm	Lieut DAVIES returned from FLAT IRON COPSE.	
		8 pm	Capt. ROWBOTHAM - Capt. No 66 + "D" Section that Sub-division returned from GREEN DUMP having been relieved by 138th Field Ambulance. Row	
	6	6 am	Captain BINNIE + 75 O. Ranks to left for Flat Iron Copse for beaux duties.	
		10.30 am	Visited FLAT IRON COPSE. Found (O.C.) Major King out up the line.	
		10.30 am	A.D.M.S. visited FLAT IRON copse + held conference re following days operations	
		12 noon	Row Capt. ROWBOTHAM in Travel B. retro Stretchers + blankets for following days operation.	
		3 pm	He returned from Ambulance train at Fin Much Roobe + returned 1.30 am 7th Oct. Row	
	7	12.15 am	2 NCOs + 30 Men 124 Inf. Bde arrived at beaux	
		1.30 am	Capt ROWBOTHAM returned	
		11.30 am	Capt ROWBOTHAM with new draft of 140 beaux division (12 men) and 64 Infantrymen as bearers all to look up the line with beaux division. No 7 Amb. No 161 or 139 Famb.	
			Lieut BURNS left for duty at 34th Inf. Bde. Copse at 11 noon hours	
			Fine - showery	
		1-5 pm	32 Infantrymen 124 Inf Bde detailed as bearers + 1 officer + 75 men 138 Field Ambulance returning for a rest to the Dump - These went for a hot bath + to prepare	
		10 pm	Major Thornton BARNES No 138 Field Ambulance bearers + my infant report details left up the line for beaux duty	

WAR DIARY
or
INTELLIGENCE SUMMARY
(Erase heading not required.)

Army Form C. 2118

Place	Date	Hour	Summary of Events and Information	Remarks and references to Appendices
Camp Reg'l.	7	12 pm	Bearer Hospital - Field Hospital in Native Bazaar	
		11 pm	We had no lights above ground but under [ground] H/Qtrs. HdQrs. H66 and Field Amb. were lit.	
	8	5am	Dr. - a very troublesome head on our left	
		6	One day preparations up. Hd. Camp - too sick from transfers from 41 Bn + 4 Re.	
			Divisions arr. - Capt. Rowbotham Veterinary from McCormicks. Fort	
		6:30am	Indian Divisions 129 & 140 Field Ambulance returns to quarters. also infantry 123/124	
		7	Heavy infantry attack 129 F.Re allowed - will Bn & some troubles gave I	
		5 pm	To manage for Me. Field Camp Veins out. Reu & cavalry return turned out.	
			To sources of attacks. 5 Cav. up. H/Q been divided 12 at WHISTLE VALLEY	
		6 am	recovered instructions field lights	Reu
			much important	
	9	9:15 am	Received instructions to send up 140 Field Ambulance bearer division 6 to at THIRTLE	
			ALLEY at 11 am to proceed to McCormick's for heavy fight.	
			The bearer Div. had a very hard day - a light enquiry + fails sent out & natives	
			drawn - field works while boy attack arr.	
		11 am	To furl 1 NCO + 60 men search 5 car govlin + 3 carts under command of Lieut. Jackets	
			sent out for THISTLE ALLEY	
		11:30 am	Made instructions received 1 in field detach. 1 to 1 NCO 16 men Bn 2/1st R.E.S. Welsh Frontier field.	

WAR DIARY or INTELLIGENCE SUMMARY

Army Form C. 2118

Place	Date	Hour	Summary of Events and Information	Remarks and references to Appendices
Camp X2gd Medical Dump	Oct 9th	1 pm	Went up to McCormicks post & found all 140t. bearer division out at Aid post-	
		4.30 pm	On way back from McCormicks post I met 3D infants detach. going up to McCormicks post for bearer duties, having just left THISTLE ALLEY. Later Iwas informed 50 infantrymen had gone up altogether at about the same time.	
		5.30 p	Returned to Camp. I found Captains HOGG & BINNIE had returned to camp from McCormicks post meanwhile.	
		6.45 pm	1 NCO & 6 men (Menzies Div. of 144t. Inf. A.T. details) returned to camp (Medical Dump) They were fed before returning to their Divn.	
		8 pm	Lieut ROCHE & 100 bearers 138 F3 Ambce returned from McCORMICKS POST.	
		9.40 pm	79 bearers 129 F3 Ambce left for McCORMICKS POST for bearer duties - Lieut HUDSON i/c as far as FLAT IRON COPSE	
		9.30 pm	138 bearer division fed & provided with food & blankets for rest. Rw	
	10th	4.30 am	Bearer Division 140t. Field Ambulance returned to Camp. Lieut HUDSON with bearer division 138t. Field Ambulance left for FLAT IRON COPSE - bearer Station gn. to McCORMICKS POST.	
		2 pm	Received orders that Iwas to hand on to OC 98t. F Amb & take on CORPS COLLECTING STATION	
		8.15 pm	E NALKING WOUNDED by 10 am 11th unit from the same offices.	
		10 pm	Bearer division 139. Field Ambulance returned to Camp for rest. Meaulte Trii Rw	

Army Form C. 2118

WAR DIARY
or
INTELLIGENCE SUMMARY
(Erase heading not required.)

Place	Date	Hour	Summary of Events and Information	Remarks and references to Appendices
Camp H.Q.	Oct 11	8.30am	Rear Division 13S. Field Ambulance returned to camp for rest.	
		9.45am	Main body 140S Field Ambulance moved out for BECORDEL and around 9.55 am 7 Field Amb FRXCORPS MAIN DRESSING STATION for WALKING WOUNDED from 30th Div	
BECORDEL WORKS COLLECTING STATION WALKING WOUNDED		10 am	Relief completed.	
		1.10 p	Rear party arrived. Weather fine. Raw. Total personnel 30 Officers & 106 other ranks. Divided roughly 1/3rd into 3 Officers 130th Ambulance Buses, moving, cleaning up & reorganising the camp — on attack by XV Corps on Eaucourt.	
	12	2.30 pm	Casualties expected to be heavy.	
		5 pm	First battle casualties arrived.	
		7 pm	Battle casualties arriving in continuous stream — Omnibuses arriving from the line Casualties 12 noon 11th to 7 1/2 hours 12th Wounded 230 Sick 62. These included Casualties from 4th 6th 9th Bth 14th 15th 21st 24th 30th 41st 47th 56th New Zealand & others (12 areas) from X Div New Zea Fus Raw	
			Weather fine. Raw Corps Hosp Raw	
	13	9 am	The heavy intake of Wounded has been caused by attacks all evening on Stuff, Schwaben, all evacuated to CCS & Corps Rest Station. 4 Then two were a block and seldom were than a charabanc load (25) fit for billets, place waiting for evacuation. Casualties 12 noon 12th to 12 noon 13th Wounded 992 Sick 67. These included casualties from 1st 2nd 4th 8th 9th 12th 15th 21st 24th 29th 30th 41st 47th 50th NZwound v2 Canadian division & Corps troops. 30th Division and 20 Sick & 438 Wounded & 29th Div Sick & 245 Wounded. 13 Div Sick & 75 Wounded	
			Weather fine Raw	
		2 pm	A visit visited camp & it appeared has the desire for more bellow the lines the area & my field ambulance would be relieved in 3 hours	
			L/Cpl B? Lieut.	

Army Form C. 2118

WAR DIARY
or
INTELLIGENCE SUMMARY
(Erase heading not required.)

Instructions regarding War Diaries and Intelligence Summaries are contained in F.S. Regs., Part II. and the Staff Manual respectively. Title Pages will be prepared in manuscript.

Place	Date	Hour	Summary of Events and Information	Remarks and references to Appendices
BÉCORDEL	Oct 14	10 am	Ambulance Cars 138 & V1243 (4 of each) which had been available during operations on 12/7/13+ NBa returned to their ambulances under instructions from A.D.M.S. 41st Div. Fine day	Rau
	15	12 noon	Handing over completed - 88th Field Ambulance (A.D.M.W.C.S.) 35th Div. took over - Total casualties stams in the Somme	O/R: Killed 1 wounded 1 ? Total 20 S
		1.30 pm	moved out for RIBEMONT BILLETS	Rau
		4.15 pm	arrived billets RIBEMONT	
RIBEMONT	16th	5.40 am	Horse transport moved out to entrain at EDGEHILL at 7 pm for BETTENCOURT - Capt Hobb in Command	Rau
		11.10 am	Personnel moved out to entrain at EDGEHILL at 2 pm to proceed to BETTENCOURT	
		12 noon	Motor Ambulance left RIBEMONT to proceed by road to BETTENCOURT	
BETTENCOURT		3 pm	Motor transport arrived BETTENCOURT Fine	Rau
	17-	1.30 pm	Personnel arrived in billets BETTENCOURT. Fine	
		7.10 pm	Horse transport arrived in billets BETTENCOURT. Raining	Rau
	18-		Raining. Showery. Cleaning up -	Rau
		3.45 pm	Jo Brigade/M(H) Hm to see Dr Major LLOYD GREENE - Sine.	
	19-		Rain. Parade for equipment checking. Personnel specials.	
		2.30 pm	Horse transport moved out to station LONGPRE to entrain for CAESTRE	
		4.35 pm	Personnel & Motor Ambulance wagon moved out for LONGPRE Station	
LONGPRE Stn	20th	7.35 pm	[Proces] after entrainment of personnel horses under command of Captain ROWBOTHAM, train left LONGPRE Station for CAESTRE & motor ambulances left spread for CAESTRE etc [Tip]	Rau
METEREN		6.50 am	arrived CAESTRE station, met by motor ambulances men from Hadfortmits of his Offer	
		7.40 am	Moved out to billet at METEREN. Personnel only	

WAR DIARY or INTELLIGENCE SUMMARY

Army Form C. 2118

Place	Date	Hour	Summary of Events and Information	Remarks and references to Appendices
METEREN	20"	9:30am	Arrived BULL METEREN with personnel from TRANSPORT arrived at BULL METEREN	
		10.30am	On this journey loading & unloading of transport was carried on by a loading part detailed from the Infantry Battalion to load & unload the whole Brigade transport. Arrangement were made to send on the dixies & breakfast rations from CASSEL Station to BULL METEREN so as to be ready to give breakfast to personnel on arrival in billets. Marched up to billets and pay. Fine, cold - frost. R.W.	
METEREN 21st		9am	Parade. G.O.C. held up inspection & visit to Sub. Ambulance.	
	22nd		Instructions rec'd to proceed to billets BOESCHEPE exit 124 bughts. Ambulance arrived in billets.	
BOESCHEPE		2:30pm	Left RENINGHELST with Captain ROTHBOTHAM to inspect the dressing station & a.d.s. P.O.C. at RENINGHELST - OUDERDOM - (Burning Motors) DICKEBUSCH (advanced d.s.) VOORMEZEELE - SPOIL BANK (A.D.S.)	
		7pm	Returned BOESCHEPE with Captain ROTHBOTHAM. R.W. Fine, cold - frost.	
			Now in billets & village - advanced part with Captain ROTHBOTHAM proceeds to OUDERDOM & takes over the Dog-out of the 2nd - - Captain HOGG and advanced part (1 N.C.O. & 4 men) left to learn working of A.D.S. at RENINGHELST. R.W.	
	23"	9am	Process marched to A.D.M.S. at FLETRE Fine - cold - frost. Capt Lewis proceeded to Chatham for Gas Course	
		4pm		
		9am	Capt Lewis with 4 N.C.O's and 10 men left to take over Main Dressing Station at Remy siding. A Sections reported to Capt Hogg at A.D.S. Lokhe	

Army Form C. 2118

WAR DIARY
or
INTELLIGENCE SUMMARY
(Erase heading not required.)

Instructions regarding War Diaries and Intelligence Summaries are contained in F. S. Regs., Part II. and the Staff Manual respectively. Title Pages will be prepared in manuscript.

Place	Date	Hour	Summary of Events and Information	Remarks and references to Appendices
Bousbecque Ploegsteert	24th Oct.	7.30am	Remainder of Ambulance left Bousbecque for Ploegsteert.	
"	25th	9 a.m.	Arrived Ploegsteert and took over Dressing station from 4th Australian Field Ambulance.	
			Busy arranging wards and dressing rooms. Car went to St Omer for supplies from British Red Cross Society.	
"	26th	6.30am	Leave opens for Ambulance. Lt Col R.C. Willmot and Dr Basson A.S.C. M.T. proceeded on leave. Captain J.A Davidson acting O.C.	
		9.30am	Went round hospital, with Engineer Officer. Handing in reports & alterations required.	
		12.30pm	Four men admitted to hospital. All books with good recommendations.	
		3 pm	Capt Davies arrived back from "the Court".	
"	27th	10 am	I visited A.D.M.S. about condition of motor Ambulances. We are one short and have one in workshops leaving two halfshots and a Ford to do work of whole Ambulance.	
			Medical Reconnaissance made of Ploegsteert, Oosttaverne, Deûlémont, Warneton dressing stations and R.A.P. by Capt. Rowbotham and myself.	
			Evacuated 30 cases of Measles from 19th Bn K.R.R.C.	
			Lieut D.G. Foley attended to 2 6"/532 R.F. for temporary duty in relief of Capt. Hodgson who is proceeding on leave.	
			Lieut. J.S. Dyson proceeded to Bousbecque in place of Lieut Foley.	
"	28th		Lt. Dyson returned to M.D.S. at Ploegsteert.	
		9.30am	Capt. Rowbotham & I attended conference on medical Reconnaissance.	
		11.30pm	52 more cases of Measles evacuated from 18th K.R.R.C.	
"	29th	10 am	Visited M.D.S. at Auckdown & A.D.S at Deûlémont. Found all in order.	
		3 pm	Attended medical conference at A.D.M S. Office	
			152 cases diagnosed as Measles from 18th K.R.R.C. now proved to be suffering from Scabies & Lice	

9

Army Form C. 2118

WAR DIARY
or
INTELLIGENCE SUMMARY
(Erase heading not required.)

Place	Date	Hour	Summary of Events and Information	Remarks and references to Appendices
Remy field	1 Oct 30th	9 am	Sent out to St Omer to get equipment from Red Cross.	
		3 pm	Capt. Davies instructed first batch of men in use of new small bore Respirator.	
			You have returned from workshop and another near in. Dressing Station byell begun have returned to work Shift. Mongo River ambulance took up position at Remyfield and it has rained every day.	
"	31st	—	Capt Davies proceeded to Berguedou & Dickebusch to instruct personnel there in use of new Respirator. Lieut Ryan relieved Lieut Gunn as A.D.S. the latter returning to Remyfield. Affairs went their accord. Completed repairs in premises proceeding slowly on account of want of material.	

J. D. Davies
Capt.
for Lt. Col. R.A.M.C.
Deputy 140th Field Ambulance

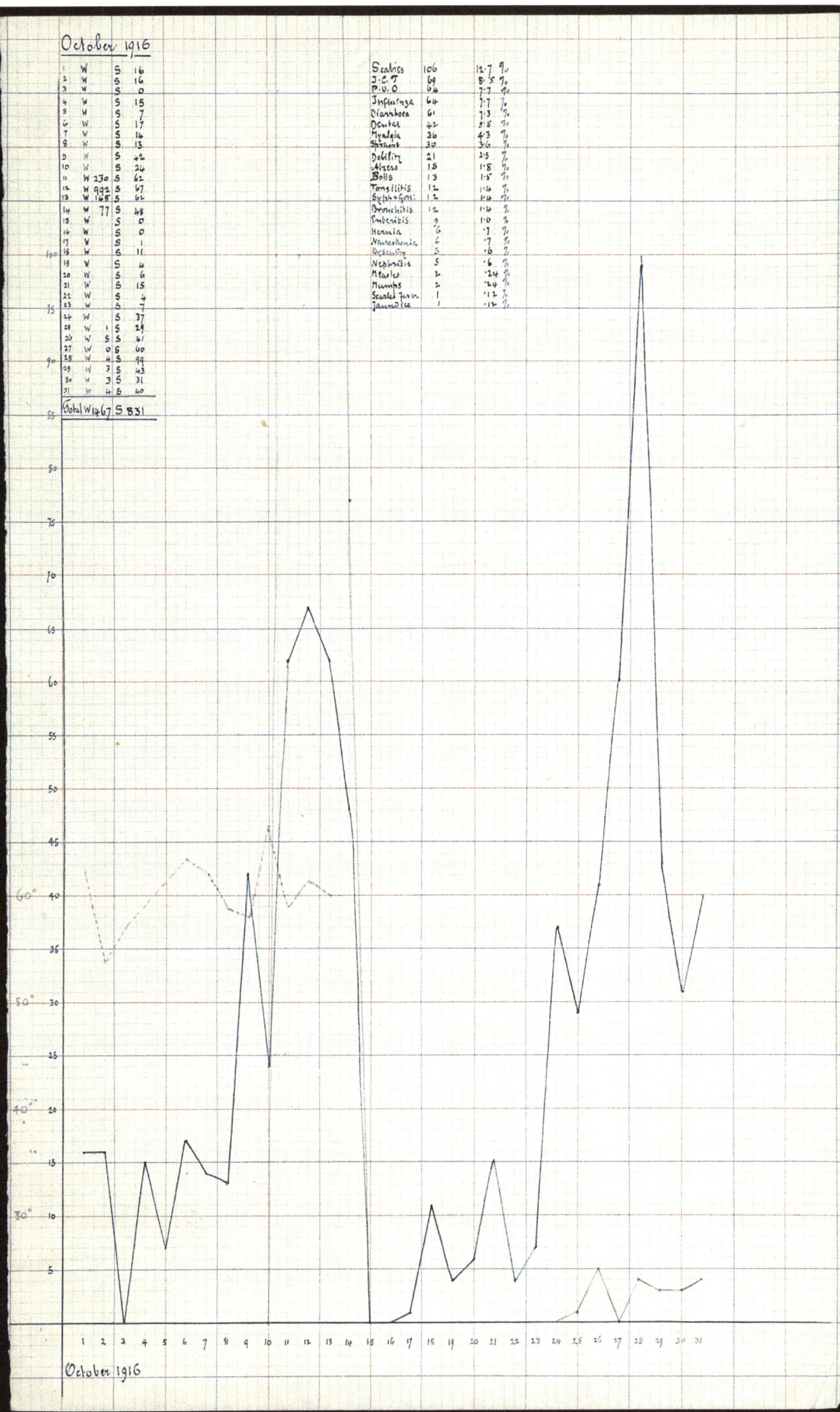

Confidential

War Diary

of

140th Field Ambulance

COMMITTEE FOR THE
[MED]ICAL HISTORY OF THE WAR
Date 13 MAR. 1917

Army Form C. 2118

WAR DIARY
or
INTELLIGENCE SUMMARY
(Erase heading not required.)

140th Field Ambulance
MEDICAL

Instructions regarding War Diaries and Intelligence Summaries are contained in F.S. Regs., Part II. and the Staff Manual respectively. Title Pages will be prepared in manuscript.

Place	Date	Hour	Summary of Events and Information	Remarks and references to Appendices
Reninghelst	1st Nov.		Capt. Davies proceeded to Abeele to draw money for pay. Men at Ouderdom & Dickebusch paid during afternoon. Men at train shewing station & bath in evening. A.S.C. instructed in use of small box respirator	
	2nd Nov		Payed Australian Engineers at A.D.S. Capt Butler A.S.C. Officer in charge of Divisional Ambulance Workshop. Division Veterinary, German Prisoners Camp & Dickebusch Fort (as arranged in exchange for a Subalt).	
	3rd "	10.30am	The G.O.C. Division and A.D.M.S. inspected the hospital. Busy evacuating sick evacuees and inspecting direct evacuee strays (war diary handed Capt Rawbadow).	
	4th "	9am	Board of enquiry held at Ouderdom on loss of Draught Mule from Resolution on Wagon. Veterinary; Capt Davies & Lieut Jones.	
		11.00am	Asst. Veterinary Officer R.A.D.M.S. re Corporal Ameroid.	
		11.30am	Lieut. Gleeson joined 12th F. Barney Regt in relief of Capt Wilson who goes on leave. Division Ouderdom	
			Personnel busy whole morning. Cook houses, Ablution huts, Refuse burner etc.	
	5th "		Returned from leave last night - midnight.	
			Busy day in Office & about the hospital & grounds with improvement	Raw
	6th "		Visited OUDERDOM - DMS 2nd army. DDMS X Corps + ADMS & Div inspected OUDERDOM & RENINGHELST main dressing stations - also P.O.W. camp OUDERDOM.	
	7th "		Air attacks last very wet Lieut JONES left unit on completion of 12 months service - No relief owing to shortage of established Medical Officers to B medical officers (123 12 A? this GADS & RAPs for left section	Raw
	8th "		Visited OUDERDOM, DICKEBUSCH.	Raw
	9th "		earth day. fine weather	Raw

WAR DIARY or INTELLIGENCE SUMMARY

Army Form C. 2118

140 Field Ambulance
MEDICAL

Place	Date	Hour	Summary of Events and Information	Remarks and references to Appendices
RENINGHELST	16	11 am	Visited OUDERDOM + DICKEBUSCH. Inspected Prisoner of War camp DICKEBUSCH – OUDERDOM. Capt. Davis proceeded on leave to England. (M/day) I became acting ADMS in Lt Col Kemp's absence.	
	12		proceeding this day to England. W. Anthony the H.Q. mess tent broken down here.	Rain
	14	11 am	Visited OUDERDOM – DICKEBUSCH & VOORMEZEELE – more artillery activity than usual. Lieut DYSON proceeded to DICKEBUSCH having been relieved by the MO battalion returning from leave.	Rain
	17		Weather has been cold the past 3 days – frost at night. Fine since the 9th inst. Unable to perform ordinary duties, very other day titrate to Report. The relief was delivered in 18th unit in DICKEBUSCH causing 13 wounded. Observing Gemache DNS returned from leave. have been in our sight since taking over on 24th Oct. Capt HOGG received military cross	Rain
	18			Rain
	20		Fine rain in evening	Rain
	21		Fine Captain Hogg proceeded on leave (10 days) Lieut DYSON left until became MO 23 "A" Middlesex Rgt	Rain
	22		To OUDERDOM in the morning	Rain
	23		Rain early, Rain, Fine later.	Rain
	24		Fine – [crossed out] SPOIL BANK, ADS since 20 Oct. Fine, Inspected aid post VOORMEZEELE Captain Danton proceeded on leave (14 days)	Rain
	25		Rain	
	26		Fine rain in evening	Rain
	27		Was a member of a Court Martial on an Army officer Lieut Stewart in the morning Circles	Rain

Army Form C. 2118

140th Field Ambulance
MEDICAL

WAR DIARY
or
INTELLIGENCE SUMMARY
(Erase heading not required.)

Place	Date	Hour	Summary of Events and Information	Remarks and references to Appendices
RENINGHELST	28		Fine & dry.	
	29		Fine & dry. Rev Lieut Housley reported for duty. Fine & dry. Revd Lieut Housley. Saw about making roads at MDS Reninghelst.	
	30		The casualties during the month have been very slight. Scabies & trench fever have been a slight feature. CTD not known in Brigade. Frost bite have been noticed chiefly in the battalion in line centre - see footnote. [chart attached hereto Appendix 7.]	7

Rawnsley
Lt Col OC 140th Field Ambulance.

November 1916

Appendix 7.

Day				
1	S 36	W		4
2	S 57	W		1
3	S 52	WW		1
4	S 36	WW		0
5	S 56	WWW		3
6	S 36	WWW		1
7	S 42	WWWW		1
8	S 36	WWWW		1
9	S 52	WWWW		1
10	S 44	WWWW		1
11	S 31	WWWW		1
12	S 25	WWWW		2
13	S 34	WWWW		1
14	S 34	WWWW		1
15	S 33	WWWW		0
16	S 42	WWWW		13
17	S 37	WWWW		0
18	S 31	WWWW		2
19	S 30	WWWW		2
20	S 34	WWWW		0
21	S 35	WWWW		0
22	S 43	WWWW		0
23	S 45	WWWW		1
24	S 29	WWWW		0
25	S 24	WWWW		1
26	S 44	WWWW		4
27	S 32	WWWW		3
28	S 37	WWWW		2
29	S 16	W		0
30	S 39	W		0

Total Sick = 1125
" Wounded = 48
Daily Av. Sick = 37.5
" " Wd = 1.6

Disease	Count	%
Influenza	175	15.5%
P.M.O	149	13.2%
Dental	97	8.6%
I.C.T	85	7.4%
Myalgia	48	4.2%
Diarrhoea	36	3.2%
Boils	30	2.6%
Trench Feet	28	2.4%
Bronchitis	25	2.2%
Nephritis	25	2.2%
Ametropia	21	1.8%
Enteritis	18	1.6%
Impetigo	17	1.5%
Tonsilitis	16	1.4%
Sprains	13	1.1%
V.D.H + D.A.H	13	1.1%
Hernia	10	.88%
Contusions	9	.8%
Albuminuria	8	.7%
Pleurisy	6	.5%
Synovitis	5	.44%
Neurasthenia	4	.35%
Mumps	2	.17%

Dotted pencil line = Temperature
Ink line = Sick
Pencil line = Wounded.

Degree F. Mean Reading of 3 taken at 6 a.m. 2 p.m. 9 p.m.

C27.   A.D.M.S   Secret

Herewith War diary for the unit
for month of November.
Also Operation Orders No 7-13 inclusive.

Rayment
Lt
10no9amb.

1/xn/16.

Dec. 1916

41st Div.

140/1943.
Vol 8

Confidential

War Diary
of
140th Field Ambulance

From 1st Dec:16
to 31st Dec:16

Volume VIII

COMMITTEE FOR THE
MEDICAL HISTORY OF THE WAR
Date 13 MAR. 1917

WAR DIARY or INTELLIGENCE SUMMARY

Army Form C. 2118

140th Field Ambulance   MEDICAL.

Place	Date	Hour	Summary of Events and Information	Remarks and references to Appendices
RENINGHELST	1916 Dec 1	11 am	Conference of Field Ambulance Commanders at A.D.M.S. Office – (Notes)	
	2	2 pm	Sergeant Major ROBERTSON. R.A.M.C. left the unit for duty with 134 Field Ambulance. Cold – Frost. Rev	
			Inspected DICKEBUSCH A.D.S. & afterwards OUDERDOM M.D.S. Cold – Frost.	
			Sergeant Major PILGRIM R.A.M.C. reports for duty from 134 Field Ambulance in exchange for S/Major Robertson. Weather cold & frost. Rev	
	3		Cold. Fine weather. Rev	
	4		Milder. Fine morning – rain afternoon. Rev	
	5		Held a board of examination for a commission for a Pte – Rev. Rain	
	6	9.30 am	O.C. Divisional Train inspected Sanford Wells Field Ambulance.	
			Read Rounds & saw 123 Machine Gun Company re inoculation. 128 Ay 49C above & jones on tea tube (Water Supply) at DICKEBUSCH. Lieut RICHARDSON ✗ to 163 Fd Amb reports for duty. Fine weather	
	7		Gallant inspection (weekly) – Captain DAVIES returned from leave & sent to OUDERDOM M.D.S. in exchange Captain ROWBOTHAM left for leave (10 days). Lieut HENSLEY to A.D.S. DICKEBUSCH. Rev	
	8		W.L. Day. A.D.M.S. inspected horses – Lieut FOLEY left for duty with 47th Division. Rev	
			Visited Wounded DICKEBUSCH & OUDERDOM – Captain ROWLAND reported from 47th Division for duty in exchange for Lieut FOLEY. – Lieut GAINE to DICKEBUSCH A.D.S. for duty Rev	
			Fog. A.D.M.S. inspected unit on parade & morning station RENINGHELST. Rev	
			Snow.	
			Inspected OUDERDOM – DICKEBUSCH. VOORTIEZELE. TOUR BANK. in morning. dull weather. Rev	
	12		Board of examination held for orders advancement to 4/100 for RGA Arranged for evacuation from R.A.P. VOORTIEZEGGE & A.D.S. DICKEBUSCH to be carried out by FORD Car Motor of hope ambulance from Indian Cavalry. Rev	
	14		Board of Examination for Commission for Officer in Indian Army. Rev	

Army Form C. 2118

WAR DIARY
or
INTELLIGENCE SUMMARY

140th Field Ambulance
MEDICAL.

(Erase heading not required.)

Instructions regarding War Diaries and Intelligence Summaries are contained in F.S. Regs., Part II. and the Staff Manual respectively. Title Pages will be prepared in manuscript.

Place	Date	Hour	Summary of Events and Information	Remarks and references to Appendices
RENINGHELST	1916 Dec 15	9/15	Viva voce examination for cooks – walked into Churchgate. Rau ADMS weekly conference	
	16	11	To CHIPPEWA – LACLYTTE baths – DICKEBUSCH ADS – VOORNOZEELE – BULLDARK – OUDERDOM. Men paid fair frost – Visit MORRISON went to HAZEBROUCK for weeks course in sanitation	
			Captain ROWBOTHAM returned from leave & took over duty at M.D.S. OUDERDOM from Captain DAVIES, Rau who proceeded on divisional extra school for two weeks system – heavy snow forecast. Rau	
	21		Frosty weather the past three days –	
	22		Rain the past two days – inspected DICKEBUSCH A.D.S. Rau	
			Rain in morning, frost after	
	25		GOC inspected M.D.S. REMINGHELST in morning	
	26		GOC inspected horses – fine dull frost – Pte Boulthornard was wounded in DICKEBUSCH on a lorry returning from R.A.P. VOORNOZEELE about 4 pm. – Fine hut.	
	27		Warmer dull – inspected OUDERDOM M.D.S. – R.T. Page (?) wtn was wounded at VOORNOZEELE	
		3pm	3 casualties from accident at 123 Inf Byr, brought about Rau – Caused to & from at Divisional school in Sanitation & found feet	
	28	Bot	Visited C.O Rev of Field Ambulance equipment. Rau	
	29		C.O Reinforcement found	
			Inspected OUDEROOM – DICKEBUSCH – VOORNOZEELE TOIL SWA. – BEDFORD HOUSE – Prevalence of very cold enemy artillery action. trained with unit – Mud – wind – heavy rain at night – new	
	30		Mud cloudy – Thick fog have been less prevalent – a lot albuminuria & nephritis – PUO & Influenza but no serious disease. Infective rabies prevail – monthly chart	Appendix R.
	31		5 casualties from a strike mortar accident at training school in OUDERDOM	

R.C Murray Lt. Col OC 140th Field Ambulance

C43   A.D.M.S   Confidential

Herewith war diary for this unit
for December 1916 please

1/1/17

[signature]
o/c
2/140 ? amb

December. 1916

1	S	25	W	0
2	S	43	W	0
3	S	23	W	0
4	S	38	W	0
5	S	27	W	2
6	S	36	W	1
7	S	36	W	0
8	S	29	W	0
9	S	33	W	0
10	S	24	W	0
11	S	38	W	2
12	S	40	W	0
13	S	42	W	3
14	S	38	W	1
15	S	29	W	1
16	S	30	W	2
17	S	28	W	0
18	S	45	W	2
19	S	32	W	0
20	S	41	W	1
21	S	42	W	2
22	S	39	W	1
23	S	36	W	0
24	S	34	W	2
25	S	10	W	0
26	S	39	W	3
27	S	46	W	5
28	S	36	W	1
29	S	28	W	8
30	S	24	W	1

Total Sick = 1025
" Wnd = 39

Appendix 8

Influenza	= 147	= 14.3 %
Dental	= 109	= 10.6 %
P.U.O	= 84	= 8.0 %
Myalgia	= 65	= 6.3 %
I.C.T	= 65	= 6.3 %
Neph: + Album:	= 60	= 5.7 %
Bronchitis	= 48	= 4.4 %
D.A.H + V.D.H.	= 30	= 2.8 %
Boils	= 27	= 2.6 %
Diarrhoea	= 25	= 2.4 %
Lacer: and Cont:	= 22	= 2.7 %
Optical	= 21	= 2.0 %
Impetigo	= 14	= 1.3 %
Tonsilitis	= 14	= 1.3 %
Pleurisy	= 12	= 1.1 %
Abcess	= 10	= .9 %
Syph. + Gon:	= 10	= .9 %
Sprains	= 9	= .85 %

Enteritis	= 8	= .7 %
Hernia	= 8	= .7 %
Synovitis	= 8	= .7 %
Trench Feet	= 7	= .65 %
Trench Fever	= 6	= .55 %
Mumps	= 1	= .09 %

Ink line ——— = Sick
Pencil = Wounded
Dotted Pencil = Mean Daily Temp:
taken at 8.0 a.m
2.0 p.m
9.0 p.m

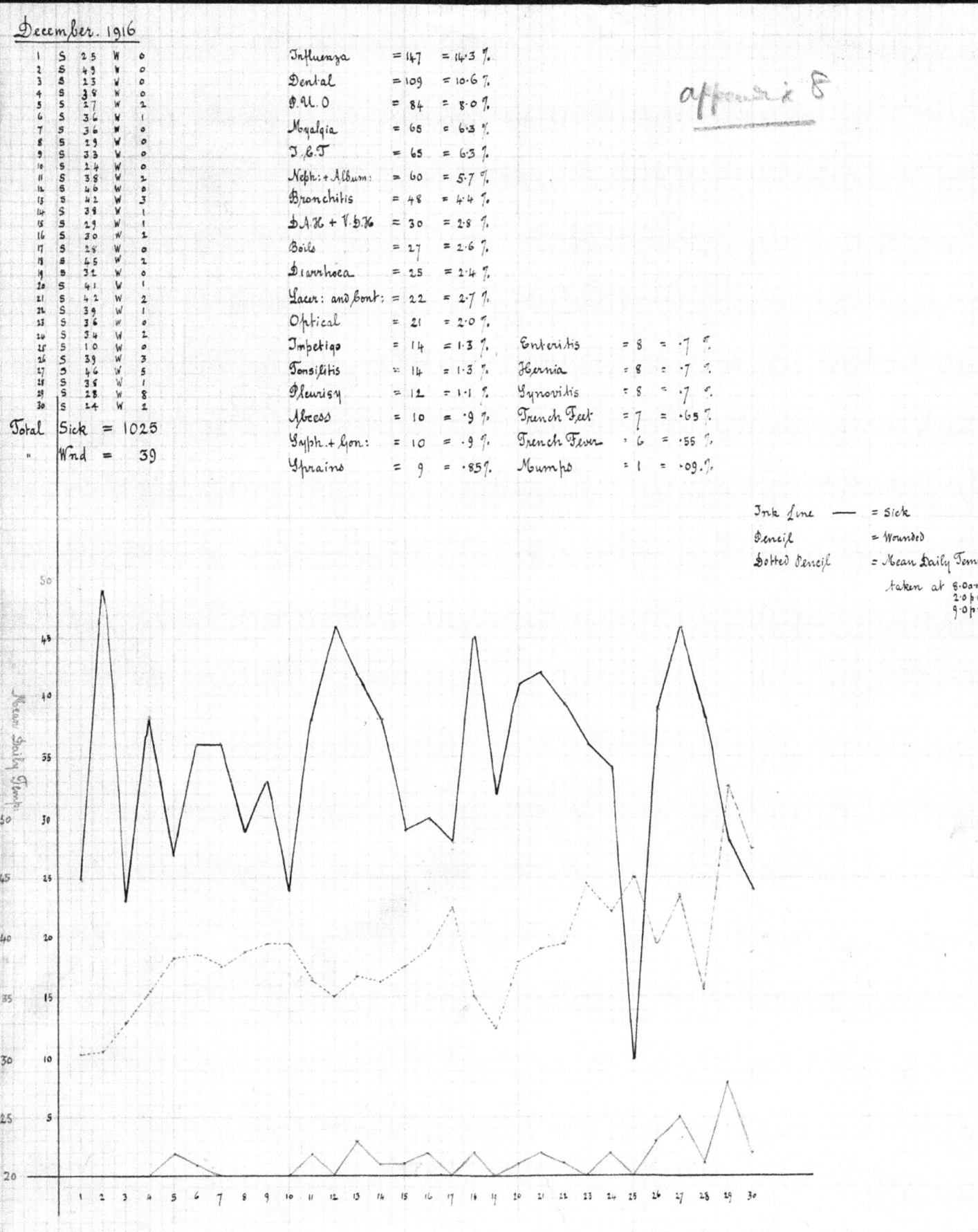

Confidential

War Diary

140th FIELD AMBULANCE R.A.M.C.

From Jan 1st 1917   To Jan 31st 1917

COMMITTEE FOR THE
MEDICAL HISTORY OF THE WAR
Date   13 MAR. 1917

Army Form C. 2118

WAR DIARY
or
INTELLIGENCE SUMMARY

140th Field Ambulance MEDICAL.

(Erase heading not required.)

Instructions regarding War Diaries and Intelligence Summaries are contained in F.S. Regs., Part II. and the Staff Manual respectively. Title Pages will be prepared in manuscript.

Place	Date	Hour	Summary of Events and Information	Remarks and references to Appendices
RENINGHELST	1917 Jan 1st	12.30 pm	The Weather continues very mild - 'Finis' Inspected Train during visit to OUDERDOM attended a lecture at BAILLEOL, with two other officers of the unit, on Horse Management by Colonel HOBDAY RA.	Rcw
		3 pm	Finis rain - mild	
	2		Lieutenant GAMM proceeded to A.D.S. DICKEBUSCH & Captain Davies returned to headquarters.	
	3		Finis rain - mild. Inspected the balloon at RENINGHELST for shelter of patients in event of hostile shelling. Arranged for RAP's & BEDFORD HOUSE to be inspected every other day by an officer from the A.D.S. Stock taking of the Ambulance Equipment continued.	Rcw
	4	9 am	Weekly parade & inspection by self of personnel - Gas drill performed in my presence - Stock taking nearly complete except one or two items not at present available -	Rcw
	5	11 am	ADMS Conference. Orders received to take over DRS from 138th F.Amb. from 7th Gt. inst. inclusive	Rcw
	6	10 pm	Captains STEW & BINNIE 138th F.Amb. with Lt & Qr Mr DODDS came over relating over to I/Kews	Appendix 8
			then personnel OUDERDOM M.D.S. & DICKEBUSCH A.D.S.-	Rcw
		6 pm	Lecture at Headquarters of Field Ambulance by Captain GOSSE RAMC on "RATS."	
	7	9 am	SPOIL BANK RAP, VOORMEZEELE RAP, BEDFORD HOUSE personnel relieved by 138th F.Amb personnel & proceeded to RENINGHELST headquarters. An advance party 1 NCO & 12 proceeded from headquarters to WIPPENHOEK.	
		2 pm	Proceeded to DRS WIPPENHOEK & arranged taking over of the same -	Rcw
	8	10 am	OC 138 F.Amb came re relief - The relief of OUDERDOM, DICKEBUSCH & RAP's above constituting the evacuation of the line was completed - 'B' section complete proceeded to DRS WIPPENHOEK.	
		1.30 pm	Proceeded to YPRES en route to RAP's held up by shelling in YPRES for over 1hr at the ASYLUM.	Rcw

Army Form C. 2118

WAR DIARY
or
INTELLIGENCE SUMMARY
(Erase heading not required.)

140th Field Ambulance
MEDICAL

Place	Date	Hour	Summary of Events and Information	Remarks and references to Appendices
NIPPEN HOEK	1917 Jan 9	1pm	Completed relief - mild weather - SLEET. all relief satisfactory.	Appendix 9
	10		GOC the Army inspects division but NOT D.R.S. Rev Spent day in cleaning up camp - Found D.R.S very full of patients & had to arrange for evacuation GOCX Corps & DDMS X corps inspected - Found Sn6 (?) (anomoment at D.R.S. b, Divisional troops CRUMPS) Rev	
	11	9	Colder. Sleet. Held my weekly parade.	
		9.30am	ADMS held weekly PR &TO 'Board. Rev	
	12	11am	A.D.M.S weekly Conference - asked for more Ambulances & blankets for D.R.S	
		3pm	Attended lecture at HAZEBROUCK on EYE TROUBLES & NIGHT BLINDNESS. a very good discourse - No cause assigned for the night blindness but generally believed famine Rev	
	13		Showed - Entertainment at DRS by divisional funeral string band - Rev	
	14		Capt Frost Captain HOGG left for temporary duty with 26th Royal Fusiliers -	
	15		1 NCO & 1 man examined for skilled mechanics at STEENVOORDE. Rev Lieut GAMM took on medical charge of 11th Royal WEST KENTS vice Captain McKIRICK to 140 Field Ambulance	
		5pm	Russian Prison Working part at VOORMEZEELE. This part is now reduced to 76. Rev To ADMS office with Captain ROWBOTHAM.	
	16		Sergeant WILKINSON left to take a temporary infantry commission The Corps School of Sanitation invited to show the DRS Sanitation to the students, as a model camp.	
			Sergeant Major YORKE ASC reports for duty vice Sergeant major DUGGAR for duty with the divisional train. Captain McKIRICK evacuated to CCS Debility & mental condition Rev	

WAR DIARY or INTELLIGENCE SUMMARY

145th Field Ambulance — MEDICAL

Army Form C. 2118

Place	Date	Hour	Summary of Events and Information	Remarks and references to Appendices
NIPPE & Ex	1917 July 19		Heavy fall of snow. Pte Hanrahan taken to light railway duty.	
	20		Captain Davies proceeded to Lt. Queens for temporary duty during absence on leave of M.O.	
		11.30	R.M.S. Curry proceeded to HAZEBROUCK for instruction for day in School of Cookery.	
		12.30 pm	General Lushington acting G.O.C. division inspected	
	21		Sergeant Lawson from 6th A inspected -	Ren
	22		2 N.C.O's proceeded to Sable for a week's course of instruction in the treatment of scabies -	Ren
	23		Lieut Hensley proceeded to HAZEBROUCK for 2 weeks course of instruction in Sanitation. Sergt Manson attended for interview with G.O.C. on applying for an infantry commission	Ren
	24	5pm	Spent a lecture at the divisional School on Sanitation	Ren
			Went round to VOORMEZEELE & SPOIL BANK to inspect the morning part with Captain Rowland.	Ren
	26		Weather has continued very cold & tents nightly -	Ren
		3pm	Brigadier Towsey act. Divisional Commander inspected	
			A.D.M.S weekly conference.	
	30		Received operation order prepare for operations.	
	31	11am	Confcce with A.D.M.S. and Field Ambulances at A.D.M.S office - The admissions of sick has increased the past two weeks to considerably higher than normal for the D.D.S. This is chiefly accounted for by fevers of uncertain origin & myalgia. The number of cases of jaundice is the only exception after the hot summer days when fever in general. A weekly parade of personnel has been held on Thursdays & myself & daily by the Sergeant Major. A.D.M.S confcce of field ambulance Commanders has been weekly on Fridays at 11am & the A.D.M.S	

WAR DIARY
or
INTELLIGENCE SUMMARY
(Erase heading not required.)

Army Form C. 2118

Place	Date	Hour	Summary of Events and Information	Remarks and references to Appendices
WIPPENHOEK	1917 Jan 31		has attended here weekly on Thursdays at 9.30 am to whom See cases recommended for P.B. in T.O. & Trench feet if any. Trench feet have been few. I.C.T. has been still prevalent on all feet. The boys, but especially feet due to boots getting hard & putting no damch. The feet cases are the most difficult as they are unable to be returned to duty until proper heels, taking all the cases as fit is quite a few days – The severe weather has no doubt caused a higher rate Sickness but the rate of admissions will number & precursors of the commoner diseases, daily mean temperature attached – about

R.C. Wilmot
d aut
seuro faun | Appendix 11. |

Secret.

Appendix 8

140th Field Ambulance. Operation Order. No 14. Copy No: 2.

Reference O.S. Maps   5a 1/100.000
                                27 1/40.000
                                  28 1/40.000

1. The 140th Field Ambulance will be relieved by the 138th Field Ambulance.

2. Relief to commence at 10a.m. on 7th January and will be completed by 4 p.m. on the 9th January.

3. On completion of relief 140 Field Ambulance will be responsible for the Divisional Rest Station at WIPPENHOEK.

4. An advance party from 138 Field Ambulance will arrive at OUDERDOM on 7th January at 10 a.m.

5. This party will be distributed as under.

    1 Officer and Batman
    1 N.C.O. I/Ch.
    1 Nursing Orderly   at DICKEBUSCH   A.D.S.
    1 Cook.
    4 G.D. Orderlies

    1 Water duty orderly   at DICKEBUSCH   H 28. a 2.3.

    4 G.D. Orderlies
    1 Nursing Orderly   at VOORMOZEELE   R.A.P.
    2 Water duties

    3 Bearers   at BEDFORD HOUSE.
    1 Nursing Orderly

    4 G.D. Orderlies   at SPOIL BANK.

    1 Clerk   at OUDERDOM.

6. O.C. "B" Section will relieve a like number of personnel at these stations, with the exception of:—

    1 N.C.O. at DICKEBUSCH

    1 G.Duty orderly at each VOORMOZEELE,   BEDFORD HOUSE, and   SPOILBANK

    1 Water Duty at VOORMOZEELE.

    1 Clerk at OUDERDOM.

7. Personnel of "B" Section on relief will proceed to RENINGHELST M.D.S.

    Total. 1 Officer (Lt. Morrison) 18 Other ranks.

8. CAPT. DAVIES with advanced party 1 N.C.O. and 23 O.Ranks will proceed to WIPPENHOEK. Parade 9 a.m. Full marching order.

9. Unconsumed portion of the days ration will be carried in each case.

10. The advanced party 140 Field Ambulance will be accompanied by a limber which will return the same day to RENINGHELST.

11. The advanced party will make themselves acquainted with the working of the D.R.S. No stores will be taken over or handed over by the advanced party.

12. Orders for Main body will be issued later.

6 January. 1917.
   Issued at

R. C. Wilmot
Lt. Col. R.A.M.C.
Commanding 140th Field Ambulance.

Copy No 1   File.
      2   War Diary.
      3   O.C. "B" Section
      4   O.C. "C" Section
      5   Capt. Davies. (O.C. Advance Party)
      6   A.D.M.S. 41st Division
      7   A.D.M.S. 47th Division.
      8   122 Infantry Brigade
      9   123 Infantry Brigade.

140 Field Ambulance. Operation Order No 15 Copy No 2

Appendix 9

Ref O.S. Maps 5a. 1/100,000
             27 1/40,000
             28 1/40,000

1. The relief of 140 Fd. Ambulance by 138 Fd. Ambulance will be completed to-morrow. 9th inst.
2. The 140 Field Ambulance will leave RENINGHELST M.D.S at 9 a.m.
3. A Rear Party composed as under will be left at RENINGHELST
        Capt. ROWLAND
        Q.M.S.
        13 Other Ranks.   1 Limbered Wagon.
4. The rear party will complete the handing over of equipment and clean up the camp.
5. All Army and Red Cross Stores will be handed over.
6. Unexpired portions of the days rations will be carried.
7. Capt. ROWBOTHAM will take over the Army and Red Cross Stores at WIPPENHOEK.
8. Receipts will be obtained for all stores handed over
9. Acknowledge.

January 8th 1917.
Issued at. 17.45

Copy No 1   File
        2   War Diary
        3   Capt. ROWBOTHAM.
        4   Capt. ROWLAND
        5.   A.D.M.S 41 Div
        6   "   41 Div
        8   122 Inf. Bde.
        9   123 Inf. Bde.

R.Arnust
Lt Col RAMC
O.C 140 Fd. Ambulance

Appendix 10

Operation Order Note — Appx No 2

1. From this date the Divisional Rest Station will receive all the sick of the division.

2. Cases not likely to be fit within 7 days will be transferred to [CCS].

3. The Orderly Officer will warn [inform] ward cases obviously not going to recover within 7 days. Such cases will be sent on to CCS [as soon as] a [convoy cart] is ready.

4. The Recreation Rooms will be used for all minor cases but beds or stretcher cases after wards are filled.
The accommodation of recreation rooms is to be taken as 36.

5. The D.R.S. will be kept at its recommended [strength]. The orderly officer will arrange to transfer to CCS the requisite number of cases to keep the numbers [below its] normal [level of] accommodation. If it becomes [too] overcrowded, [notify after the] daily admissions at 6 p.m. to [—]
Copy No 1 — [ADMS Div]   Lieut Col
         2 — War Diary   [signature]
         3 — [OC RS?]
         4 — OC [field]   [no sent at]
         5 — [ADMS? of Div]

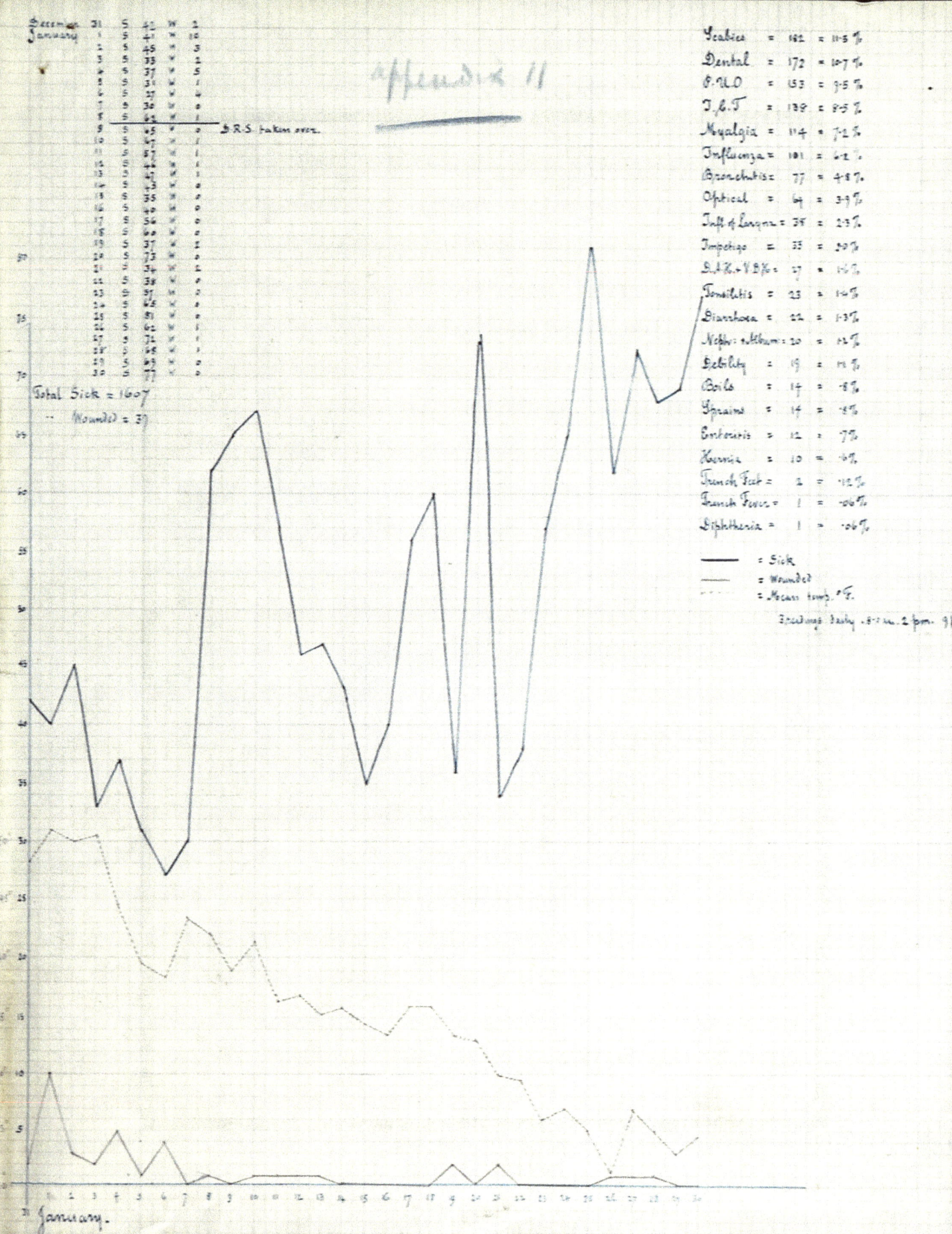

Confidential. 149/2042 Vol 10

A.D.M.S.

W. Wear

110 tt Field Ambulance

COMMITTEE FOR THE
MEDICAL HISTORY OF THE WAR
Date 11 MAY. 1917

WAR DIARY
or
INTELLIGENCE SUMMARY
(Erase heading not required.)

Army Form C. 2118

140th Field Ambulance
MEDICAL

Place	Date	Hour	Summary of Events and Information	Remarks and references to Appendices
WIPPENHOEK	1917 Feb 1		LT. & Q.M. R.G. WHITNEY arrived. Unit has been for four months without a Q.M. during which time Q.M.S. CURRY has ably performed many of Q.M's duties	
	2		LT. COL WILMOT arranged to No 2 Canadian C.C.S suffering from ? pneumonia. An officers mess is commenced. CAPT. F. ROWLAND assumed temp. command of unit. At 8 a.m. thermometer registered 26° of frost this being the lowest temperature recorded by us so far.	ZM
	3		Weather still very cold - Sunday. improvements in camp proceeded with	ZM
	4	9.15	A.D.M.S. inspected camp	
		5pm	Working party recalled from VORMEZEELE by A.D.M.S. in hut horses some 28th health appeared owing to shortage of water due to frost, especially in baths	
	6	11.30 am	LT. HENSLEY left for temporary duty with 11th QUEENS. 10th Regt. W. Kents	
	7	10 a.m.	P.M. dene made on 11936 Pte. MILES 19th MIDDLESEX when died accidentally in hospital yesterday. Cause of death pneumonia. CRUMPS gave sound with performance bound on men recommended P.B. and T.B.	
	8	9.30 a.m.	A.D.M.S held wound weekly Board	ZM
	9	3 pm	Attended monthly meeting of Army Medical Society at REMY SIDING Wounds of joints	ZM
	10		A.D.M.S conferance Ambulances were drawn from YPRES for first time for some weeks	

WAR DIARY
INTELLIGENCE SUMMARY
(Erase heading not required.)

Army Form C. 2118

Place	Date	Hour	Summary of Events and Information	Remarks and references to Appendices
WIPPENHOEK	11	3 p.m.	LT. COL WILMOT returned from 2nd Somme then P.C.S. Moor to the Asylum	
			& Neir (?) for BOESCHEEPE & about 10pm to billets near	
	12		CAPT. ROWBOTHAM (?) to about another course at HAZEBROUCK	
	13	6.45 p.m.	2/2 LONG FLD AMB. arrived here for one or two days	
	14		CROMPS gone some odd 3 entrenchment	
	15		LT.COL WILMOT held med. 3 hour for A.E.	
	16		CAPT. DAVIDSON to X CORPS CAVALRY for ??	
			CAPT. ROWBOTHAM returned from another course at HAZEBROUCK	
	18	10.30	LT. COL WILMOT (?) to Inspection of new ?? was (our act. in ??)	
			?? (impre) community one to the ??? from the	
			??? CAPT. ROWBOTHAM for A.D.M.S. L.OF C. in A.	
	19		?? visited camp No/088/99 Lt. MURRAY R.E. & while & ??	
			R.A.E. HESDIN to blow up left immunition. R.F.C.	
	20		74092. Pte STONE was sent to base as unsuitable employment	
			for under active command	
	21	9.30	R.A.L. AND Lieut ?? & CROMPS just back from	
	22		Sunday service. Lieut ?? to PR. ??	
	23	2.30	?? Medl. mate of Army No.?? to HAZEBROUCK meeting at 7.30. got back	
			to camp 10 evening ditto to X Brigade & met our Common. ?? ??.	

WAR DIARY
or
INTELLIGENCE SUMMARY

(Erase heading not required.)

Army Form C. 2118

Instructions regarding War Diaries and Intelligence Summaries are contained in F.S. Regs., Part II. and the Staff Manual respectively. Title Pages will be prepared in manuscript.

Place	Date	Hour	Summary of Events and Information	Remarks and references to Appendices
WIPPENHOEK	1917 Feb. 24	9.30 a.m.	Exchange of motor ambulances and personnel completed. 86905 Lce. Cpl. TILBURY left for England to attend cadet course. D.O.i/c this hand gave permission to CAPT. ROWBOTHAM to hand over temporary duty with D.A.C. CAPT. HENSLEY returned from temp. duty with 10th Mob. Boat Park.	
	25		CAPT. ROWBOTHAM evacuated to No. 10 C.C.S. suffering from neuralgia of sciatic nerve.	
	26		T4/210598 Dr. JONES H.B. to HAVRE on own muncher.	
	27		T.A.B. inoculation of third proceeded with.	
	28	6 a.m.	LT. MORRISON left for England on transportation of extract. 9 lorries sent for loading from YPRES returned and two loads of bricks drawn from rooms used and the number of patients admitted has generally month has been a busy one. The number only is that in excess of any other number. Types of disease who have been exposed to from abnormally severe weather. Number of deaths on admission with number & percentage esophuasal and number of scabies same S. Attached - chart of admissions with number and car temperature increases of the common diseases and death rate in field ambulance.	Appendix 12

J. Rowland Capt. A.D.C. 140 in Field Amb.

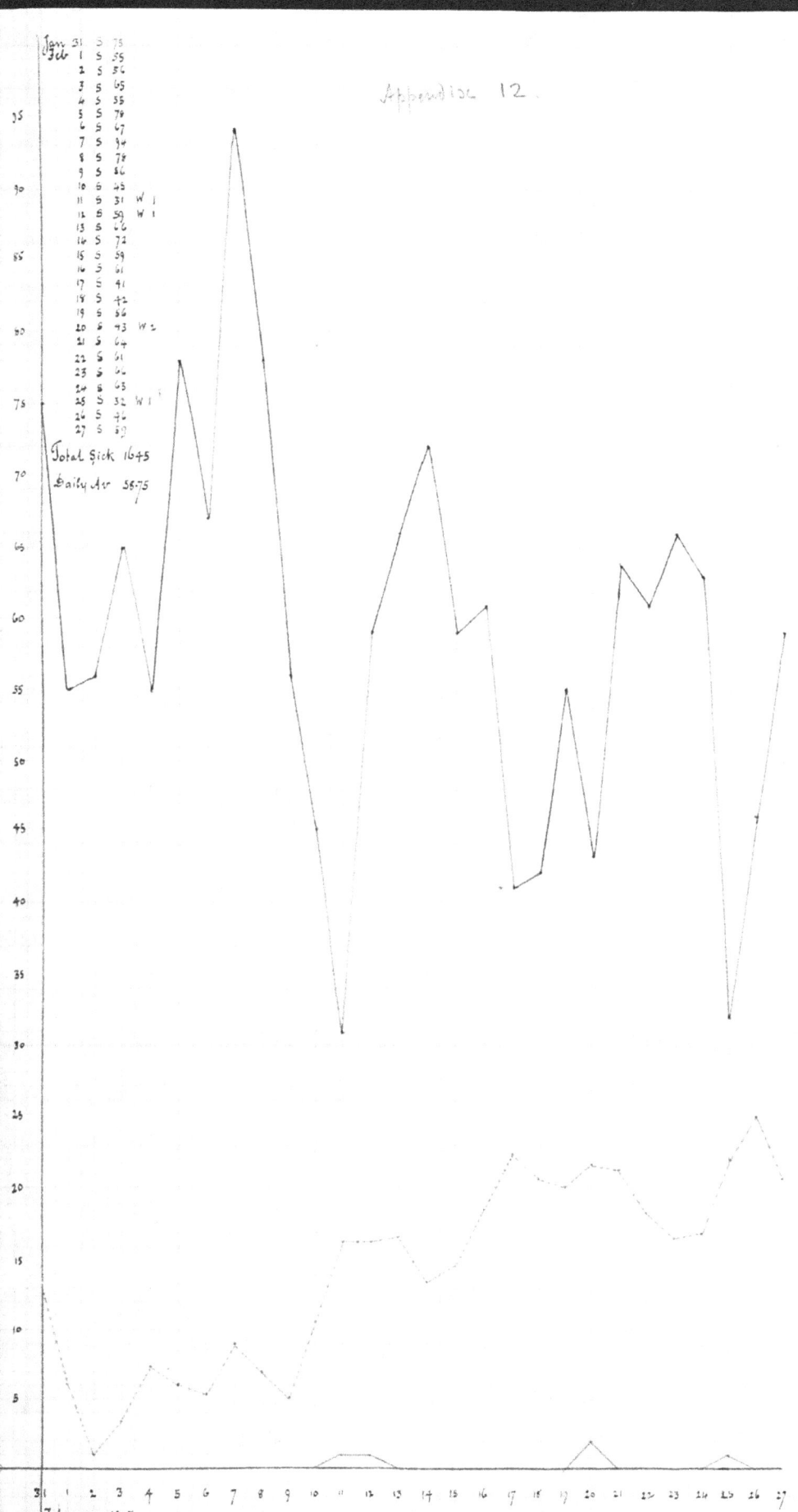

Appendix 12.

Confidential 140/2042

Vol XI

War Diary

140th "Field Ambulance"

1st March 1917
to
31st March 1917

COMMITTEE FOR THE
MEDICAL HISTORY OF THE WAR
Date 11 MAY 1917

MEDICAL WAR DIARY or INTELLIGENCE SUMMARY

140th Field Ambulance — Army Form C. 2118

(Erase heading not required.)

Instructions regarding War Diaries and Intelligence Summaries are contained in F.S. Regs., Part II. and the Staff Manual respectively. Title Pages will be prepared in manuscript.

Place	Date 1917	Hour	Summary of Events and Information	Remarks and references to Appendices
Wimereux	1		Body of Driver A.H. Smith T4/057483 A.S.C. was removed to 10 C.C.S. for Post Mortem examination. Summary of evidence was taken and forwarded to A.D.M.S. Weekly Board was held by D.A.D.M.S.	272
	2		Pads of Moore Hut course of instruction of Army Med Corps at HAZEBROUCK	
	3		CAPT HOGG detailed for 14th M.A.B. CAPT HARRISON reported for duty	
	4	11.15	CAPT ROWLEY A.T.C. attached off strength on secondment to base	
	5		Memo cards of Smiths in France A.D.M.S. wanted account	
	6		63770 Pte KNIGHT J.E. struck off duty with 14th Div Supp Col A.S.C. for desertion M.R.A.M.C. duties	
	7		Case of measles (Pte KNOWLES) occurred amongst R.A.M.C. personnel	
	8		Pte 90370 Pte POWELL A.C. detailed for 22nd M.A.C. for duty as clerk Weekly med board held by D.A.D.M.S.	
	9		Sitting meeting of nos. 1/3 Sec of RAILFUL Stretcher Squad of Bearers held. Bar made death of Dr SMITH R.E. Provided Lt Col of corpse	
	10	11.0	Member CAPT ROWLANCE Lt HEADLEY CAPT HARRISON remained for RIGR.	
	11		Board of Enquiry with gun ammunition proceedings + evidence of Mission held Lt Col WILLMOT	
	13	6.30	47th A.E.C. band party of Scotch & Guard performance	277
	14		Influenza from leave yesterday. The Wagon park for Walk cases was finished and a few made with Re Wagon park for ambulance + G.S. Wagons. Wanted to build with fare.	

R.C.W.

MEDICAL WAR DIARY 140th Field Ambulance
INTELLIGENCE SUMMARY

Army Form C. 2118

Place	Date	Hour	Summary of Events and Information	Remarks and references to Appendices
NIPPENHOEK	1917 Dec 15	9.30 am	held weekly Board of P.B. & TB men. Weather fine colder. Sick in DRS high - 267 above time frakens. A.D.M.S Conference cancelled. Fire - cist - progress with garden satisfactory. Seeds on order - Had two hopper windows put in each I hut for better light & ventilation - RW	
	16.			
	17	9.50 am	A fire broke out in the Quarter Master Stores - a certain amount / damage - about 1/5 has done to Stores. The store was canvas with a wood frame - The canvas was destroyed - little damage was done to the frame due to the expedition & efficient manner in which the fire was tackled - The fire was extinguished by 10.12 am all the Quartermaster receipts were burnt - at the time of the fire, no fire was in the store - There was no building near - The fire started on the roof - Anti-aircraft guns were firing with a regular bombardment at the time at which the fire took place - Neither fire - asked for Court Inquiries on the fire - RW I went to Rumishkot to see ADMS & CRE. Arranged for fault for windows doors & camouflage - Plus & orders taken for windows & stove for Nissen hut which is now erected & left without these additions by RE. Arranged for Lieut Stansley to be MO 3rd Labour Corps Middlesex Regt in addition to his other duties. RW	

MEDICAL WAR DIARY 140th Field Ambulance   Army Form C. 2118

INTELLIGENCE SUMMARY

(Erase heading not required.)

Place	Date	Hour	Summary of Events and Information	Remarks and references to Appendices
WIPPENHOEK	1917 Nov 19	10 am	DDMS & the ADMS inspected the camp – Captain W.L.A. HARRISON proceeded to 12: B: E Surrey Regt. for temporary duty during absence on leave of M.O. Had personnel huts made with better ventilation by having boards off, which has been fitted on our ventilation holes (reversed). Had on better type moveable louvre put on to fire buckets. Rew. The sick are decreasing daily. Figure now 213.	
" 20.			Arranged to have the personnel's huts whitewashed inside. The billeting Munitions boots was lost from the cyclist's pocket – the cyclist was later beaten from him – yet the wind keeping very high – Rew.	
21	5 pm		Gave a lecture at the divisional School on Organisation (Medical) in the field & in attack & defence – Cont. for sun was here on fire of Qu Stone on 17. in H.Q. ale numerous outside the work. Cold. Rew	
22			Captain DAVIES returned from temporary duty with entrenching Battalion – weather cold & hard. Pte MINNES a patient under arrest broke out of hospital. Brought in 27 h. was apprehended. No Conference by ADMS	
24			Weather cold & fine – started wiring up road which was much cut up by rain – Had details cleaned out & holes frozen kept moist for ablution Sheds Cookhouse Rew	
"			Sick now down to 183 – Clock put back 1hr at midnight 24–25.	

Army Form C. 2118

MEDICAL WAR DIARY 140th Field Ambulance
or
INTELLIGENCE SUMMARY
(Erase heading not required.)

Place	Date	Hour	Summary of Events and Information	Remarks and references to Appendices
NIPPENHOEK	1917 Mch 26		Cold & fine — Had the rest of the tents made fly proof — Rev	
	27		Cold & fine — Gas in progress — Cannot overcome in & come positions front & rain did not favor the gardening — difficulty in getting cobbles ment. Lieutenant E.A.V. HENSLEY to 32nd R. Fusiliers vice Captain GRIEVESON to 140th Field Ambulance. Sick rate the past few days 2 or 3 in hospital — Scabies & numerous past two days 7 & 10 wk lad 1.2 or 3 in Unit — Scabies and still transferred to No 50 Hazebrouck, not more than 10 daily — Dental admissions have run to 17 & 18 the past three days (daily), usually about 10. Rev.	
	28		Ordinary sick is not increased. No Conference — not. Received warning order to move to training area about 5th April. Rev. During the month the work done on the DRS is as follows. Fencing the Wt. — making a wagon stand — improving the road — making two extra hoppers fallens & roads, with mud — making the near side flyproof — finishing roof of cookhouse funshel & cork of 5 huts fireplace - erection of a Nissen hut shaped disinfector & making a window in the cook house — the hut & fetters with hot supplies camouflaged & painting of woodwork & whitewash of roofs laid — A garden has been dug & R.E. & Pioneers huts & plants with vegetables about an acre planted with vegetables. List of NORM huts to N Main Road for Div ENSch — attached about 50 men left to N Main Road for Div ENSch —	
	29			
	30			
	31			13

Rawley Lt

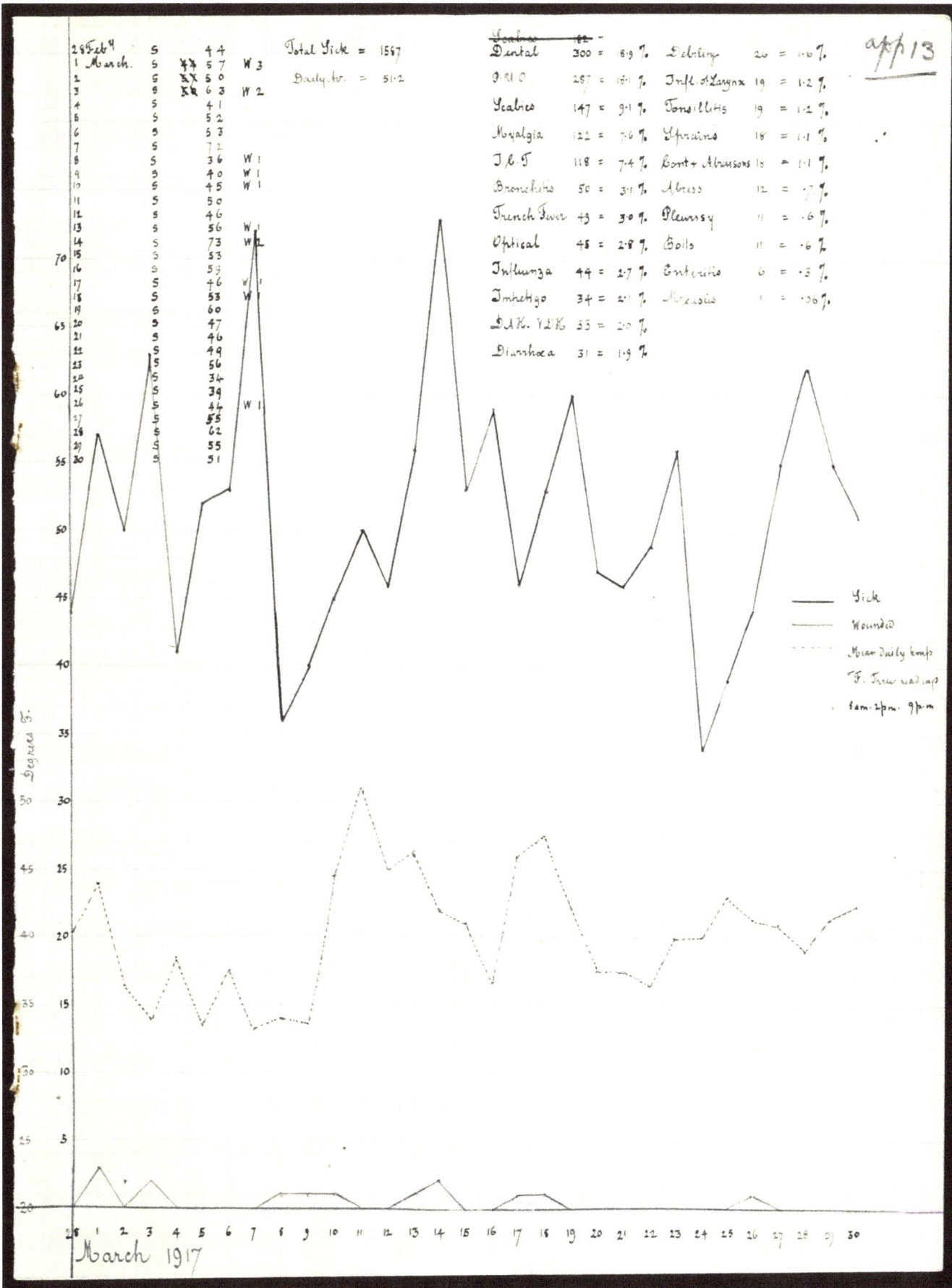

Medical

140/036

SM/2

Confidential
War Diary
140th Field Ambulance
R.A.M.C.

From:-
April 1st 1917.

To:-
April 30th 1917

COMMITTEE FOR THE
MEDICAL HISTORY OF THE WAR
Date 6 JUN 1917

Army Form C. 2118

MEDICAL WAR DIARY
140th Field Ambulance.
INTELLIGENCE SUMMARY
(Erase heading not required.)

Instructions regarding War Diaries and Intelligence Summaries are contained in F.S. Regs., Part II. and the Staff Manual respectively. Title Pages will be prepared in manuscript.

Place	Date	Hour	Summary of Events and Information	Remarks and references to Appendices
WIPPENHOEK	April 1.		Weather continues very cold. A snow storm last night.	
	3			Appendix 14
	5	4 p.m.	An advance party 139 Field Ambulance arrived to take over D.R.S. Surgeon General Porter & Lt Col Stevens RAMC inspected the camp.	Appendix 15
	6.	12.10 p.m.	Handed over DRS to 139th Field Ambulance. Moved out for STEENVOORDE with Field Ambulance En route to EPERLECQUES for training with 123 Inf. Bde. Strength 6 Officers (including Q'Masters) - 170 O.Ranks - RAMC + ASC complete less 1 motor ambulance car, 1 motor bicycle + drivers.	
STEENVOORDE	7	3.40 p.m.	Arrived STEENVOORDE men in billets in barns, officers in houses - horses picketed & wagons parked on sidings. Cold & heavy showers. March continued with Brigade to NOORDPEENE	Appendix 16
NOORDPEENE		11.15 a.m.		
		3.30 p.m.	Captain N.A. HARRISON returned to unit from 1st E. Surrey Rif. for duty arrived NOORDPEENE - went East - Roads good condition - fine day for marching - ASC in Barn near church. Officers billeted in chateau - RAMC men in school.	Appendix 17
EPERLECQUES	8	9.25 a.m.	Moved out with Brigade for EPERLECQUES. Captain GRIERSON took over No 10 OCS Elfsinghem arrived EPERLECQUES in chateau of Madame GIVENCHY - Weather clear - fine roads - good for marching - had a long halt for dinner 12.30 pm to 1.20 pm 1 mile E of WATTEN. No stragglers on march. The men are billeted with the CHATEAU - Officers in billets in cottages near by -	
	9	4.30 p.m.	The CHATEAU is unfurnished - in a bad condition & sanitary arrangements not good - The horses are in stables + out houses + wagons parked in stable square. A room on ground floor is used for a sick ward for the sick of the Brigade - The chateau is also occupied by a detachment of 130th Field Ambulance who are looking after the sick of the Army School of Musketry from TILQUES.	Appendix 18

Rev.

Army Form C. 2118

MEDICAL 140th Field Ambulance

WAR DIARY or INTELLIGENCE SUMMARY

(Erase heading not required.)

Instructions regarding War Diaries and Intelligence Summaries are contained in F.S. Regs., Part II. and the Staff Manual respectively. Title Pages will be prepared in manuscript.

Place	Date	Hour	Summary of Events and Information	Remarks and references to Appendices
EPERLECQUES	April 15		Training carried out according to programme attached – the first week by Sections – The past few days were cold with rain & sleet showers – 5th & 6th days fine – 7th day Sunday. Rained steadily all day.	R.C.W.
	12	11am	ADMS visited & saw men at training.	
	16		Field day W/EPERLECQUES used for officers to gain tactical scheme & men trained in Stretcher bearing & searching ground. Communication between RAPs & ADS faulty.	
			Walked him in morning – rain later.	
	17		Field Ambulance worked by Sections with battalions & ran found W/of MORINGHEM moving to pain the scheme was postponed & ambulance worked on found alone, arriving back in camp 12.45 pm – battn were arranged for about 100 men at HOULLE	
			The battns are in wate hutment at a farm, 100 militia away – walk is continually Yummy & at length burnt heat.	
	18		Very wet – Field day again postponed. day given up to lectures & indoor work.	
	19		Dull but fine – Ambulance by Sections worked with battalion over PIHRINGHEM found M.O's battalion moved forward too soon – in communication from 1st RAPs before advance to RAPs was not kept, after that touch was lost with MO battalion in all cases.	
	20 & 21st		Field Ambulance worked with Brigade as a whole over the same ground on Saturday 19th. Temp 48° at 8am operations concluded about 12.30 pm each day – Parade 8am each day – lectures on return to camp about 3pm – officers dinners –	R.C.W.

1875 Wt. W593/826 1,000,000 4/15 J.B.C. & A. A.D.S.S./Forms/C. 2118.

WAR DIARY

MEDICAL 140th Field Ambulance

INTELLIGENCE SUMMARY

Army Form C. 2118

(Erase heading not required.)

Place	Date	Hour	Summary of Events and Information	Remarks and references to Appendices
EPERLECQUES	22.			Appendix 19
	23.	7.50 am	Moved out for return to RENINGHELST area with transpt. Rear 1 tent subdivision "C" section with Captains DAVIDSON & DAVIES. W/T Orders & Load afor 122 Inf Bde attd	
			Nil to Cassel and for training leaving RENINGHELST 25th. Weather fine.	
NORD PEANE		3.7 pm	Arrived NORDPEENE same billets as outward journey.	
	24	9.50am	Moved out for STEENVORDE	app x 20.
		3.15 pm	arrived STEENVORDE - long halt for dinners at 12.00 pm.	
	25	8.15am	moved out en camp the RENINGHELST - LACLYTTE Road, 6 Camp intended for progress of Mess is now prepared by use as a Corps Main dressing station for walking & wounded.	app x 21.
		1 pm	Arrived in camp.	
		3.30 pm	A.D.M.S. Visited Camp.	
		6 pm	I.A.D.M.S. tree about arrangement for camp - Weather but for most of march.	
	26.		Busy in fixing up the camp - Roadway of surface for about 100 yards has pavement & carted to the camp from a road about ½ mile away. a new road is in course of construction through the camp - a large quantity of wire entanglements went removed & a barbed wire fence put around an adjacent field which is taken into the scheme - Buildings are being called for	
	27.			
	28.			
	29.			
	30.		use for their was purposes Cookhouses ablution shed latrines Urinals v incinerator are being built. The original camp was roughly 200 x 360 feet & the new field is a rough Quadrilateral of 320 x 360 feet. The administration front is additional to this. The above being available for accommodation & bivouacs for personnel.	

WAR DIARY or INTELLIGENCE SUMMARY

Army Form C. 2118

MEDICAL 140 Field Ambulance

(Erase heading not required.)

Instructions regarding War Diaries and Intelligence Summaries are contained in F.S. Regs., Part II and the Staff Manual respectively. Title Pages will be prepared in manuscript.

Place	Date	Hour	Summary of Events and Information	Remarks and references to Appendices
Camp Kemmel-beek Proven	24/9/20		From 3 am 24th to 4 am 26th heavy intermittent shelling in the area around the camp. Shots near the camp. No one about 20 yards. Attended to statement casualties. Case moved in the county May & 196 patient. Men made appendix 22. R.C. Marsh, Lt Col. ROR France	App 22

Appendix 14.

142 Field Ambulance. Operation Order No 14. Copy No. 2

1. This Field Ambulance will be relieved by 139 Field Ambulance on April 6th.
2. This Field Ambulance will proceed by route march to GANSPETTE area. Packs will be carried by lorries under arrangements made by division.
3. An advance party 139 Field Ambulance will be sent to this D.R.S. on April 5th. The working of the hospital and offices will be explained to this party, and Officers in charge of wards will give any information necessary concerning the patients to the Officer in charge of this advance party.
4. The men on Water duty (3 in number) at outlying water posts
    viz. 2 at GODWAERDSVELDE Sh 27 S.E. R2 c 8 9
         1 at ABEELE Sh 27 N.E. L33 b 3.9
    will be relieved from personnel of the advance party of 139 Field Ambulance, as well as 1 cook and 1 G.S. Wagon with horses and driver at Corps School of Sanitation and 1 Water Cart at RENINGHELST (attached to Divisional Train).
5. The Quarter master will arrange for all inventories of Red Cross Stores, Medical Stores, Medical Comforts, and Area and other stores to be prepared in readiness for handing over to the incoming unit. Only mobilisation equipment and such other equipment as has been drawn on General Routine Orders will be carried. On handing over, receipts will be obtained and 41 Division. ACT. 7/56 will be complied with.
6. The Working party at DICKEBUSCH will be relieved on the morning of the 5th April by a party of the 139 Field Ambulance. A G.S. Wagon will be sent to arrive DICKEBUSCH 11.30am to carry the packs of the men of this Unit to D.R.S. This wagon will also bring the

shovels and picks belonging to the Unit.
7. On arrival in the new area, this unit will be responsible for collection, treatment and evacuation of personnel sick from the Brigade Group.
Evacuation will be to No 10 Stationary Hospital, ST OMER by Divisional Ambulance Cars.
8. Orders for march will be issued later.
9. Acknowledge.

3 April 1917

Issued at 6 pm

R.C.Wilmot
Lt Col RAMC
O.C. 140 Field Ambulance

Copy No. 1 File
2. War Diary
3. 138 Field Ambulance
4. 139 Field Ambulance
5. A.D.M.S.
6. O.C. "A" Section
7. " "B" "
8. " "C" "
9. Quartermaster
10. 123 Inf. Bde.

passing a village, the Unit in rear must be warned to prevent the latter entering the village.

8. O.C. "C" Section will be responsible for the transport and treatment of sick of column falling out on line of march.

9. No man will be allowed to fall out on the line of march, unless he is in possession of a chit stating his number, rank, name and initials, unit and reason for falling out, which must be signed by an Officer.

10. O's/B Sections will have Progress Reports stating condition of men and position of Unit ready for handing to O.C. 140 Fd. Amb. at 10.50 a.m., and 11.50 a.m. and subsequently at 2 hour intervals till they reach their destination.

11. Rations for the 6th and 7th will be drawn in the usual manner. Preserved rations for the 8th will be drawn on the 7th from Divisional Supply Column Dump on CASSEL ROAD (West of STEENVOORDE). Refilling point on 8th inst will be at LE NENEGAT, about ¾ mile N.W. of NOORDPEENE. On 9th inst. and onwards refilling point will be at Cross Roads 1½ miles W. of MOULLE, on main ST.OMER – NORDAUSQUES Road. The supply wagons of the Train will march in advance of the Column each day, and will rejoin at the end of the march after refilling at 8.0 a.m. on the 8th, at 8.0 a.m. on the 9th and afterwards at 9.0 a.m. daily

12. Ordnance will be delivered in the GANSPETTE Area twice weekly, on Tuesday and Saturdays by lorry. Dumping place will be notified later.

140 Field Ambulance Operation Order No 18   Copy No 2   Appendix 15

In continuation of Operation Order No 17

1. Capt DAVIES accompanied by L/Cpl RAINSFORD will report daily to the Staff Captain 123 Infantry Brigade at the billeting rendezvous which will be detailed daily in the March Table. Rendezvous for Friday 6th April. BANDSTAND, STEENVOORDE. 10 a.m.

2. L/Sgt HOLDEN with section cooks and cooks cart will proceed to STEENVOORDE at 9.30 am, April 6th reporting on arrival to Capt DAVIES and will have dinner prepared for the personnel of the Unit at 2.30 p.m.

3. Blankets will be handed in daily to Quartermaster for packing in baggage wagons of Sections. Each man will be responsible for the folding and labelling of his own blankets and handing them in at least two hours before the parade.

4. Officers are responsible that their kits will be ready for packing on wagons at least two hours before parade.

5. The Field Ambulance, less billeting party and cooks, will parade in full marching order at 12 noon April 6th outside the pack stores, and Wagons on Wagon park, moving off at 12.10 p.m to join the column at L 33 d 8.3 (Sheet 27) at 12.30 pm. Motor transport attached, in charge of Sgt Beck will leave D.R.S at 2.0 p.m and report on arrival.

6. Watches will be synchronised daily at 7 a.m.

7. Units will observe the usual clock hour halts. They will not however halt in villages. Should it be necessary to halt immediately after

13. Acknowledge.

Date.   5 April 1917
Time.   2030

R. C Wilmot
Lt Col. RAMC
Commanding 140 Fd. Amb.

Copy No 1   Filed
     2   War Diary
     3   O.C 'A' Section
     4   " 'B'   "
     5   " 'C'   "
     6   Lt + Q.M.
     7   A.D.M.S.
     8   123 Inf. Bde.
     9   139 Fd. Amb.

Copy No	File
2	War Diary
3	O.C. "A" Section
4	" "B" "
5	" "C" "
6	Lt QM.
7	A.D.M.S
8	143 Inf Bde.

Appendix 16.

140 Field Ambulance. Operation Order No 19 Copy No 2

Reference Map HAZEBROUCK. 5". 1/100.000.

In continuation of Operation Order No 18.

1. 140 Field Ambulance will continue its march with 141 Infantry Group on April 7th. Destination NOORDPEENE.

2. The transport under 2/QM WHITNEY will parade in the RUE DE L'EGLISE at an hour to be arranged later, probably 9.20 a.m. with head of column facing the GRANDE PLACE joining the Brigade transport column in rear of Machine Gun Corps.

3. L/Sgt HOLDEN and section cooks will march with transport and prepare dinner immediately upon arrival at billets.

4. The billeting party will meet an Interpreter at Road junction N. of P in NOORDPEENE at 11.30 a.m.

5. The Field Ambulance, less transport and personnel detached above will parade in RUE DE L'EGLISE facing East at 11.5 a.m. ready to march off at 11.15 a.m. 7th April.

6. Bread and cheese rations will be carried by all.

7. Motor transport will travel via CASSEL and will leave the GRANDE PLACE at 2.15 pm under Sgt BECK.

8. Brigade Report centre will close at STEENVOORDE at 9.20 am and re-open at NOORDPEENE at 10 p.m. Reports meantime to be sent to head of Brigade Group.

9. Acknowledge.

Date 6th April 1917

Issued at 20.30 hrs.

R C Wilmot
Lt Col. RAMC.
Commanding 140 Fd. Ambulance.

L/Cpl Whitney for the purpose of indicating route to
transport
1st Acknowledge –

Date   7 April 1917

Estimated 9.20 pm

R C Wilmot
Lt Col.
O C R'd Fusil

Copy No 1   3rd
       2   Var Brig
       3   O C W Section
       4   "B"
       5   "C"
       6   Lfam
       7   Afam
       8   12 DLI Left flk.

appendix 17

140 Field Ambulance Operation Order No 20 Copy No. 2

Reference Map. Hazebrouck 5a 1/100,000.

In continuation of O.O. No 19.

1. 140 Field Ambulance will complete its march with 123 Inf Bde
Group to EPERLECQUES on April 8th 1917. Route
LEDERZEELE — WATTEN.
2. The billeting party will be at the billeting rendezvous, the
Church EPERLECQUES at 11 a.m.
3. The Field Ambulance less billeting party and transport with
exception of Cooks cart and A Section Water Cart will parade
in the Chateau Drive at 9.25 a.m. ready to move off at
9.35 a.m. and the head of the column will pass the Cross Road
South of the WORD in LE MENEGAT at 9.46 a.m. in rear of
123 M·G·C⁰ and T.M.B
                    under command of L/ami Whitney
4. The transport less Cooks Cart and Water Cart will parade
in road outside Chateau with head of column opposite
Chateau Gate at 9.30 a.m. ready to move off at 9.50
and will pass cross roads S. of the Word E in LE MENEGAT
at 10.2 a.m. in rear of transport belonging to 123 M·G·C + Tr
5. There will be a long halt for dinner from 12·50 p.m — 2·20 p.m
6. Units will march in threes + not in fours.
7. Steel Helmets will be carried by all ranks.
8. Bows + cheese rations will be carried by ASC pers. only
9. One Blanket per man will be carried by G·S· Baggage Wagon
10. Corporal ORFORD + two men will be detailed to load lorry.
11. O.C "C" Section will drop a guide where the field and
leaves the main column with instructions to report to

Appendix 18.

Programme for Training

1st Week

	7 to 7:45	9 to 1	2 to 4:30
1st Day.	Squad & Gas Drill.	Stretcher exercises, practical demonstration 1st aid in Field.	Unloading equipment, examination of panniers and explanation of contents.
2nd Day.	Physical Drill including doubling & obstacle races.	Route March. (without pack.)	Tent pitching and preparing tents for patients.
3rd Day.	Company Drill.	Stretcher exercises with wounded, Lecture- Geneva Convention, to all ranks.	Equipping, loading & unloading ambulance waggons, & pourvoirs G.S. Waggons & mules.
4th Day.	Stretcher Drill.	Route March. (with packs.)	Packing & loading field ambulance. (Gas helmets to be worn for ½ hour of this exercise.)
5th Day.	Physical Drill.	Stretcher exercises with wounded, collection & transport with & without Gas Helmets.	Practical instruction in making of Latrines, Urinals, Cookhouses & method disposal of refuse.
6th Day.	Company Drill.	Route March. (with packs.)	Tent pitching and preparing tents for patients. (Officers Tactical Schemes.)

of Field Ambulance.

5-0. To 5-45

Lecture.	O.C. Field Ambulance.	Officers & Other ranks.	Scope and object of Training
Lecture	O.C. Field Ambulance.	Officers & Other ranks.	Organization of a Field Ambulance.
Lecture.	D.A.D.M.S. (do.)	Officers & Other ranks.	The Regimental Medical Service.
Lecture.	O.C. Sanitary Section (do.)	Officers & Other ranks.	Conservancy in the Field
Lecture.	O.C. Field Ambulance.	Officers & Other ranks.	First Aid in the Field.
Lecture	O.C. Field Ambulance	Officers & Other ranks.	The Working of a Field Ambulance.

Football matches, Sports &c. will be arranged for each day to commence at 6 pm

Programme of Training

2: Week

	7 to 7.45	9 to 1	2 to 5	4.30
7th (Monday) day	Company Drill	"Field Day" (Officers Tactical Schemes)		
Tuesday 8th day	Stretcher Drill (with patients)	Searching for wounded, transport over obstacles and rough ground	Preparation of bivouacs and shelters for wounded and personnel	
Wednesday 9th day	Company Drill	"Field Day"		
Thursday 10th day	Stretcher Drill (with patients)	⎱ "Field Days" ⎰ Collection, treatment and classification of wounded. Hand seats and improvised carriage of patients.		
Friday 11th day	Practical demonstration of defensive gas measures	Establishment & advanced dressing stations and methods of communication between forward and rear medical units		
Saturday 12th day	Stretcher Drill (with patients)	Formation and movements of Field Ambulance	Stable management, transport, etc. (Practical demonstration of horses, vehicles and harness by S.M. York)	

✕ (It is hoped to arrange for work with the Brigade on these days. Special attention will be paid to the subjects mentioned)

2 Field Ambulance

	5 - 0		5 . 45	
Lecture	O.C. Field Ambulance	Officers	Discipline, appointment, field messages, reports and returns.	
do	Capt Davies	Officers and Other Ranks	Precautions against Gas, etc.	
do	By Sections Section N.C.O's	Officers and Other Ranks	Rearranging and loading of wounded	
do	Quartermaster	Officers and N.C.O's	Quartermaster Duties	
do	Capt Davies	Officers and Other Ranks	Water and Bivouacs	
do	O.C. Field Ambulance	Officers and N.C.O's	Map Reading	

SECRET.   Appendix 19 Copy No. 2

140th Field Ambulance Operation Order No. 31

Ref:- Map HAZEBROUCK 5A 1-100,000

1. The 140th Field Ambulance (less details mentioned below) will march from EPERLECQUES to Prisoners Camp RENINGHELST on 23rd 24th & 25th inst.

2. An advanced party (1 NCO + 14 men 'B' Section) (Sergeant Brown) will proceed on the 20 inst. at 7 a.m. by the Sanitary lorry direct to Prisoners Camp.
   This party will take unexpired portion of the day's rations + rations for 24th & 25th also 2 Dixies. They will take 'B' Section Bag entrenching took complete.
   They will prepare the camp on arrival.

3. 'C' Section tent Subdivision with ASC(HT) attached + 3 Motor ambulance cars with drivers + 2 spare drivers + 'C' Section Cad orderlies, will remain at EPERLECQUES under command of Captain T.P. Davidson + with Captain J.L. DAVIES attached.
   This party is rationed up to 28th inst. inclusive. Rations after that date will be arranged by 122 Inf. Bde. to whom they will be attached - + who will make arrangement for their billeting in the RECQUES area.

4. The party detailed in para 3 will continue to man the dressing station — evacuations of sick as before — The daily state of sick will be rendered direct to A.D.M.S.

5. Supplies for the main body for consumption on 24th will be drawn at WATTEN on 22nd inst; Those for consumption on 25th first drawn at WATTEN on 23rd inst will be dumped by MT on 24th at STEENVOORDE. From 24th inst inclusive rations will be drawn from NIEPPENHOEK.

6. A motor lorry is allotted to the Field Ambulance for carriage of Packs & kitbags of the personnel. Two men will be left to load this wagon.

7. The Cooks cart & 'A' Section water cart will travel in rear of the unit. The remainder of the transport will march with the Brigade transport.

8. Captain N.L.A. HARRISON & L/Cpl RAMSFORD will form the units billeting party & will report daily to the Staff Captain 163 Inf. Bde. at the Billeting Rendezvous at hours named — Rendezvous for 23rd CROSS ROADS at LE MENEGAT. 10. A.M —

9. No man will be allowed to fall out on the line of march without written permission from an officer — this will state the man's number, Rank, name, initials, unit & reason for falling out —

Ambulance Car orderlies will not carry men without such written permission — The slips showing above particulars will be handed to OC No 2 Fld Ambulance, of all men carried on ambulance No first. wagons, on completion of each day's march —

10. Parade, Personnel in battle order at 7·35am in Threes & NOT Fours — To move off 7·53 am

11. Parade, Transport under Lieut WHITNEY at 7·35am to move off 7·54 am —

12. ROUTE. NATTEN to NOORDPEENE Head of column will pass Starting point Cross Roads E of NATTEN at 7·18 am —

13. Motor Transport will proceed by same road leaving EPERLECQUES 11·30 am —

14. Acknowledge —

22 April 1917
Rowley ?
O.C. 2nd ?

Issued of

Copy no 1 File
2 War diary
3 ADMS
4 123.I.B
5 I/C 'B' Section
6 — 'B' — Captain HARRISON
7 I/C 'C' Section
8 Quartermaster WHITNEY

Appendix 20
Copy No 2

140th Field Ambulance Operation Order - No 22.
Ref HAZEBROUCK 5a Trench map.

(1) The Field Ambulance will march to the STEENVOORDE area on 24th inst.

(2) The order of march for the main body is as for today.

(3) Rendezvous for billeting party is Junction CASSEL–STEENVOORDE and RYVELD–TERDEGHEM Roads 8.30 a.m.

(4) Parade. Personnel 9.30 a.m to move off 9.50 a.m

(5) Parade. Transport 9.10 a.m to move off 9.30 a.m

(6) Starting point Personnel. Road junction 50 yards South of C in WEMAERS–CAPPEL, to be passed at 10.52 a.m

(7) Starting point Transport. Railway Crossing S/of BAVINCHOVE 10.56. a.m

(8) ROUTE : Personnel via CASSEL.
Transport via CASSEL lower Road

(9) Acknowledge.

April 23rd 1917

R.C. Kenneth Lt Col
O.C. 140 F.Amb.

Copy no 1 File   4 - 123 FB   7 Q.master
         2 War diary   5. OC A Section   Issued at.
         3 ADMS   6 Captain Harrison

Issued at:
Copy No 1 File
" 2. War diary
" 3. ADMS
" 4. 123 I B
" 5 OC A Section
" 6. Captain HARRISON
" 7 Lieut. Q. M. WHITNEY.

Appendix 21 Copy No 2

140 Field Ambulance Operation Order No 23.
Ref Map HAZEBROUCK 5a 1/100.000.

(1) The Field Ambulance will march to ~~bivouac~~ Camps at CHIPPEWA on 25th instant. Personnel, Prisoners of War camp M6 a 8.8 Transport. Infantry Transport lines.

(2) The order of march is as for today.

(3) Captain HARRISON will proceed to take over the camp and transport lines. He will take 1 NCO & 2 men from the advanced party at the Prisoners camp to take over the Transport lines.

(4) Parade - Personnel & Transport 8.0am to move off 8.15 am.

(5) Starting Point. Road junction at the 6½ Kilometre mark on the STEENVOORDE - POPERINGHE Road (midway between point where frontier crosses main road & ABEELE Personnel pass - 9.23am. Transport pass 9.29am.

(6) Route. ABEELE - HILLEHOEK - R'junc Sof 2nd N in INN on POPERINGHE - ABEELE Rd then byway of crossroads 150 yards South of R in RENINGHELST.

(7) Acknowledge.

R C Wilmot
Lt Col
OC 140 F Amb.

24/4/17.

Losses to the 140 Fd. Amb. for 1 year.

Original Field Ambulance. Personnel.		Reinforcements (72 received)	
Killed	1	Killed	–
Wounded	14	Wounded	3
Sick	35	Sick	12
Transferred	11	Transferred	4
For commission	3	For commission	–
To Base. Immature	4	To Base. Immature	1
Total	68	Total	20

Grand total of losses = 88
    Killed = 1.1%
    Wounded = 19.3% (of these 2 subs. died of wounds)
    Sick = 53.4%
    Transferred = 17.0%
    For commission = 3.4%
    To Base, Immature = 5.6%

Appendix 22

14921

Vol 13

Confidential
War Diary
of
140th Field Ambulance
R.A.M.C.

COMMITTEE FOR THE
MEDICAL HISTORY OF THE WAR
Date 10 JUL. 1917

To
31st May 1917

From
1st May 1917

Army Form C. 2118
(see app. 22.)

WAR DIARY or INTELLIGENCE SUMMARY

(Erase heading not required.)

1/4oth Field Ambulance MEDICAL.

Instructions regarding War Diaries and Intelligence Summaries are contained in F. S. Regs., Part II. and the Staff Manual respectively. Title Pages will be prepared in manuscript.

Place	Date	Hour	Summary of Events and Information	Remarks and references to Appendices
Camp. KEMMEL Road M6 a 88	May 1st		Officers attended to sick & slight with near trenches (temperature) On April 29th Captain WARBSON went to temporary duty as MO to 32nd R. Fusiliers. An issue of lime juice is now being made to be drunk by all to prevent Scurvy.	app X 23.
	2nd	10 pm	Gas alarm Sounded - stood too - No gas in vicinity Sergt Smith/gas in Camp. Nothing to report.	
	5th		A.D.V.S. inspected & found horses very satisfactory & expressed himself very pleased with their condition. Sunday. The weather has been fine & hot - last week a little cooler - Today again is colder.	
	6th		Two men returned to-day from Corps School of Sanitation after a week's course of instruction there. Two men left Friday for 1st Army Rest Camp ABLETEUSE for fortnight. Work performed on the Camp during the week. (1) Material (wooden sleepers) removed for making a road through the Camp (2) Road started - about 40 yards laid - (3) Road on SE Side of camp repaired for about 40 yards - (4) Wiring in of camp practically completed. (5) Wooden floor laid in Refreshment hut. Completed on B 9 (6) Cement floor laid in Refreshment hut - " " 4 (7) Bits around Camp cleaned out (8) Urine pit dug - (9) Grease pit dug - (10) Two Latrines moved one on N.W side of Camp - one on S.E side of Camp - & floors bricked (11) Bath house which had been used as Cookhouse by previous unit cleaned out - (12) A certain number of Fire & Refuse Buckets made. R.C.W.	

Army Form C. 2118
Sheet II

WAR DIARY
MEDICAL.
146. F. Field Ambulance

INTELLIGENCE SUMMARY
(Erase heading not required.)

Place	Date	Hour	Summary of Events and Information	Remarks and references to Appendices
Camp KENNEL Road M 6 a.88	May 6.		(13) 2 Brass traps made which, owing to want of solder were unsatisfactory — also a better pattern who decided on, so have to be remade — (14) a Bridge of corduroy mats, made over the ditch from Road on SE side of camp to enable supply wagon to get to Ration Store — (15) Ration Store scrubbed out & occupied — (16) A partition fixed in Regimental hut to divide for preparing Rooms from Serving Room — & a counter fixed in Serving room — (17) a large quantity of manure in Stables taken over & wire fences & incinerator made for burning & so (on as possible) — (18) Kitchen in admin.Ration block cleaned out. (19) Leaving (the worst) — many dirs bricks from YPRES — The average strength at head quarters has been 87 all ranks — RAMC owing to working parties 51 other ranks having to be relieved once a week, one working day is lost — Bricks are drawn every alternate 3 days from YPRES 5.6.17. & then 11.12.13 & so on. Average sick in hospital or attendant has been high side about 8-10 this reducing personnel available — material collected for making own — RCW.	

140th Field Ambulance WAR DIARY

INTELLIGENCE SUMMARY

Army Form C. 2118
Sheet 3.

MEDICAL.

Place	Date	Hour	Summary of Events and Information	Remarks and references to Appendices
Camp KEMMEL Road M6a 8.8.	May 6.		ADMS inspected the Camp in afternoon. Footborn new latrine on SW side of camp — Been to small hospital marquee.	
	7.		The dump RE near camp on SW side was shelled at night. Received orders no bricks to be drawn from YPRES tonight & no transport to move after 8 p.m. British Bombardment at night. Dump shelled about midnight about 60 shells. Several casualties RE v RA. Brass Band from MONT NOIR for matim. Muster. Slight rubber Captain HARRISON left this unit for permanent duty with 23rd Bn Middlesex Regiment. Showing Cooler — Fly inspection	
	8.	3 pm	a Brassy Survey on vests & clothing landed in — Jerkins & Undercoats Fur. ADMS v DADMS inspected	
	9.	9.25 to 10.15	Bombardment in line intense + enemy reciprocates — some shells in dump.	
	10.		Divisional gas officer made a test with gas of the box respirators — some gas in closed hut + again by bombs in the open. 10 gas respirators for horses received — All horses put on dry weather. Lining & stabling cleaned up.	
	11. 12. 13.	11 a.m.	ADMS conference. fur. 15 of working party relieved — Received orders that one Tent Subdivision at NORDAUSQUES with party relieved — 122 Inf Bde would return to me here at RODTE march May 15 to 17. R.C.W. Showery. 2.5" — — — pasting relieved —	

Army Form C. 2118

Sheet 4

146th Field Ambulance   WAR DIARY   MEDICAL
or
INTELLIGENCE SUMMARY
(Erase heading not required.)

Place	Date	Hour	Summary of Events and Information	Remarks and references to Appendices
Camp Kemmel Road M.6.a.8.8.	May 13		Work completed this week:—	
			(1) Kitchen 40ft × 20 ft almost completed. Mass of wood in uprights + galvanised iron roof & walls.	
			(2) Road through camp continued — Ground prepared for laying.	
			(3) More mud removed on S.W. side of camp	
			(4) Ground near Kitchen levelled ready for dining marquee	
			(5) Incinerators + mud pit made at stables.	
			(6) Ground around Officers Quarters levelled & cleaned, manure heap removed, sand bags removed from huts + some iron sheets obtained from trench (hay) barn.	
			(7) Files at bath house emptied, cleaned & relaid.	
			(8) Ground around stables cleaned & levelled + manure burnt.	
			(9) 7 small hospital marquees "catched"	
			(10) 6 small hospital marquees pitched	
			(11) 10 bell tents for personnel pitched	
			(12) Several more pits & refuse bucket pans built.	
			(13) Several duck boards repaired —	
			(14) More sand drawn from Mont Noir.	
			(15) Several directing boards for latrines — disinfectants made about 20 to date.	
			(16) Foundations + corner pieces of two incinerators laid — kept up for base —	
			(17) Started on 1st oven in cookhouse.	
			(18) Grease trap for 1 Australian Shed completed.	
			R.C.W.	

Army Form C. 2118
Sheet 5

140th Field Ambulance WAR DIARY or INTELLIGENCE SUMMARY

MEDICAL

(Erase heading not required.)

Place	Date	Hour	Summary of Events and Information	Remarks and references to Appendices
Camp KENNELS Mba. E.A.	May 14		Fine. 11 men of working parties relieved.	
	15		3500 Blankets + 500 Stretchers for Capt Distomi MO's kit drawn from Ordnance. R.S.M. HOLDEN - Mantis took part for a fortnight's course (instruction). At 2-Area School flooded Attendance. Red Cross stores drawn from Red X Society, to Cape Guardeni Station.	
		8 am	A few sick burst in field (on E camp) adjoining this camp - 1 infantryman wounded.	
		2 pm	Received orders to send 3 nests ambulance to a detachment of 136 Pan.B on 18th inst.	
	16		For duty with 134 Inf. B85. Also in GARBETTE training area. Captain J.L. DAVIES returned from detachment with 122/B. Two 2nd class Compr/Corp - to go on course in Capt dressing Station.B. Van HCO3 Corps HUDSON + Pte WILLIAMS sent on 4 days course in Capt Par. Messing. To left for 1st Surg. field ambulance made greater Heavy showers from last night till this morning. Personnel are in 2 NISSEN huts	
	17		(Salt hatter 26) + 10 Bell Tent. Weather much colder. Byes practised for Corps Review Station Par.B. Ambulances + box reservoir received. Started filling - about 8/9 are unfit for road.	
	18	12.30 pm	"C" Section hut subdivision into lumpert returned to Camp here. Captain DAVIES & 20 OR's 141 to (temporary duty) on MO drawn, Hours + MO + 18 personnel. Also 1 Ambulance.	
	19	11 am	Byes some lines for 142.G. + forms from RE pack. Fine. Memories ...	
	20		26 men unskilled relieved. 15 men working hut relieved. Two ovens built in cookhouse.	
			1) Cookhouse building complete. 2) Road through camp continued - progress satisfactory. Rev.	

Army Form C. 2118

140th Field Ambulance

WAR DIARY
or
INTELLIGENCE SUMMARY
(Erase heading not required.)

MEDICAL.

Sheet 6.

Place	Date	Hour	Summary of Events and Information	Remarks and references to Appendices
Camp. ACEYTE ROAD Mba.S.E.	May 20.		(4) 12 Small hospital marquees erected.	
			(5) 4 Small hospital marquees pitched & trenched	
			(6) 14 bell tents pitched & trenched	
			(7) Nine sand drawn from Mont Noir for making plants for bricklaying	
			(8) Inscription boards finished & painted	
			(9) Several pits for illuminate signs bridges made.	
			(10) Started on Camps main drains, station boards trimmed of weeds.	
			(11) Two nine grease pits completed.	
			(12) Two forms for marquees made.	
			(13) Gutters for dressing tent made & put in position.	
			(14) 3 Nissen huts scrubbed out for occupation years for wounded	
			(15) The incineration nearly completed	
		30. 31.	(16) A seat fires around the Refreshment hut. (17) drew 6 beds huts from YPRES collection pts.	
			DDMS inspected the camp in morning	
			ADMS DAMS inspected camp. L.Cor.Sj Holden returns from course of instruction	
	22		Handed over 1500 blanket & 400 stretchers to 138 F.amb. 10 men Northumpark relieved by morning. – Went round ADS Dich E.BUsch – ASpk VOORMIZEELE & 4 men and posts in course of construction. CONVENT LANE – GORDON STREET – MIDDLESEX Lane.	
	23		Send a M.Manin. Screw a YMCA marquee for during Cint. interviews YMCA representative Jay.	

RCW

Army Form C. 2118

140th Field Ambulance MEDICAL

WAR DIARY
or
INTELLIGENCE SUMMARY
(Erase heading not required.)

Place	Date	Hour	Summary of Events and Information	Remarks and references to Appendices
Camp LACLYTE & MEAUX	May 24		Fine Weather. JDMS & Corps and a Major of the United States A.M.C. visited the Camp.	Sheet 7
	25	11am	Conference field Ambulance Commanders at AAMS office.	
	26		1300 V 14 men (working part) up the line. Relieved.	
	27		1300 V 14 men of party relieved. Two sick have been sent with high temperature. Pte Dawson was killed this morning with the working party by a bullet wound head. Work done during the week.	
			(1) Kitchen ovens finished building.	
			(2) Sink back floors laid in cook house.	
			(3) Our verandah finished.	
			(4) N.C.O.'s artificial manures Pluies.	
			(5) 20 ditto Pitches & Trenches in Roof fields	
			(6) 20 ditto ditto "	
			(7) Signs near finished for camp.	
			(8) x Corps S/Ca board finished.	
			(9) Reserval table & frames for dressing & receiving but made.	
			(10) Road nearly completed. Entrance improved. Sides banks. Bottomed - Surface. laid with Rubble	R.C.W.

Army Form C. 2118
Sheet 5.

146th Field Ambulance WAR DIARY MEDICAL
or
INTELLIGENCE SUMMARY
(Erase heading not required.)

Place	Date	Hour	Summary of Events and Information	Remarks and references to Appendices
Camp LA CLYTTE ROAD M16.c.8.8.	May 27.		(11) Duckboarding laid for evacuating marquees. (12) Meat safe fly-proof square shelves – fly-proof principle – also rat-proof. (13) Shelves fixed in dispensary – 4 forms fitted out. (14) Twenty fuel brackets made v families. (15) Several box drains made for patients to walk over. (16) A 60 × 30 foot YMCA marquee stained v fitted for use as dining tent. (17) Red crosses painted on roofs of 3 huts. (18) Outside 1 foot horse families – 40 × 20 feet. (19) Marquee fixed for hurricane lamps with W/D. (20) About 40 petrol tins cleaned out & painted with "W" for drinking water purposes. (21) Glazed & brick rubble collected at YPRES & brought here.	
	28	5 pm	Received orders to proceed home for substantiation for India. Orders meaning supply latched at OUDERDOM from B.I.P. unit.	
		11 pm	RE yard & area N.W. of camp shelled for several hours by Naval (?? 7.7 gun from NYTSCHAETE) about 20 casualties. (7 or 8 killed)	
	29		About inspected camp in morn. Col Sir Anthony BOWLBY – Col GORDON WATSON & Col BARLING – consulting surgeons G.H.Q. 2nd army & ? respectively visited the camp in afternoon. Weather continues fine & warm.	

Army Form C. 2118

WAR DIARY
or
INTELLIGENCE SUMMARY
(Erase heading not required.)

Place	Date	Hour	Summary of Events and Information	Remarks and references to Appendices
Camp Lachyter Rd M6 a 8.8	May 30		Hd Cooks - 1 NCO & 20 men sent to OUDERDOM for instructing parties. Bit hard to hire completely, as also to Butthouse. A run for 5 containing Mending cooker has made. 5 Sayers Stoves (No) in & there are 2 large ovens & 2 smaller ones. Sufficient for 250 & 150 meals respectively. Six Niht driers for meat. There is accommodation for 12 & there can be used. Cooking for 1600 men be provided. A latrine with 36 seats & urinal & filter is the course of the Regt. but field seats for innoculation & the complete the beds.	
	31		A funeral has been held at entrance for use of patients (wounded) on arrival a latrine has been fixed for officers - found the Nissen huts. The camp is now complete for ready. The cook & ANC men returning - Shipment - all rays. Steps being taken further & found stuff a few British - Handed over to Captain Rowland RAMC (7) on proceeding to England for duty in India. Notes chart appendix XXIV attached	29/k 24 R.C.Merrick Lt.RAMC OC 1005tems

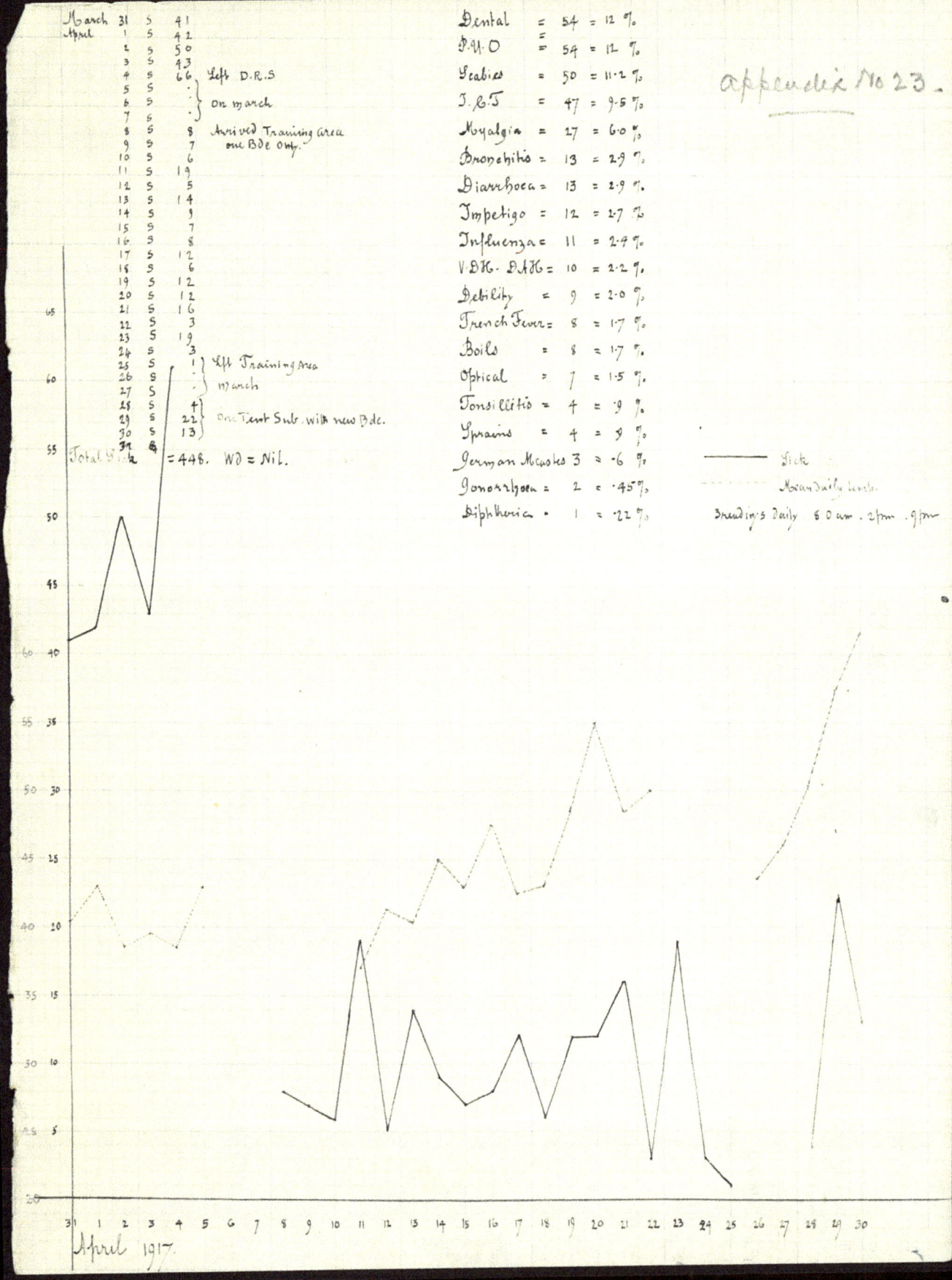

Appendix No 23.

March 31	S	41
April 1	S	42
2	S	50
3	S	43
4	S	66 } Left D.R.S
5	S	.
6	S	. } On march
7	S	.
8	S	8 Arrived Training Area
9	S	7 one Bde Only.
10	S	6
11	S	19
12	S	5
13	S	14
14	S	7
15	S	7
16	S	8
17	S	12
18	S	6
19	S	12
20	S	12
21	S	16
22	S	3
23	S	19
24	S	3
25	S	1 } Left Training Area
26	S	. } march
27	S	.
28	S	.
29	S	22 } One Tent Sub. with new Bde.
30	S	13

Total Sick = 448. W.D = Nil.

Dental	= 54	= 12 %
P.U.O	= 54	= 12 %
Scabies	= 50	= 11.2 %
I.C.T	= 47	= 9.5 %
Myalgia	= 27	= 6.0 %
Bronchitis	= 13	= 2.9 %
Diarrhoea	= 13	= 2.9 %
Impetigo	= 12	= 2.7 %
Influenza	= 11	= 2.4 %
V.D.H. D.A.H	= 10	= 2.2 %
Debility	= 9	= 2.0 %
Trench Fever	= 8	= 1.7 %
Boils	= 8	= 1.7 %
Optical	= 7	= 1.5 %
Tonsillitis	= 4	= .9 %
Sprains	= 4	= .9 %
German Measles	3	= .6 %
Gonorrhoea	= 2	= .45 %
Diphtheria	= 1	= .22 %

———— Sick
.... Mean daily Temp.

Readings Daily 8.0 am. 2pm. 9pm

April 1917.

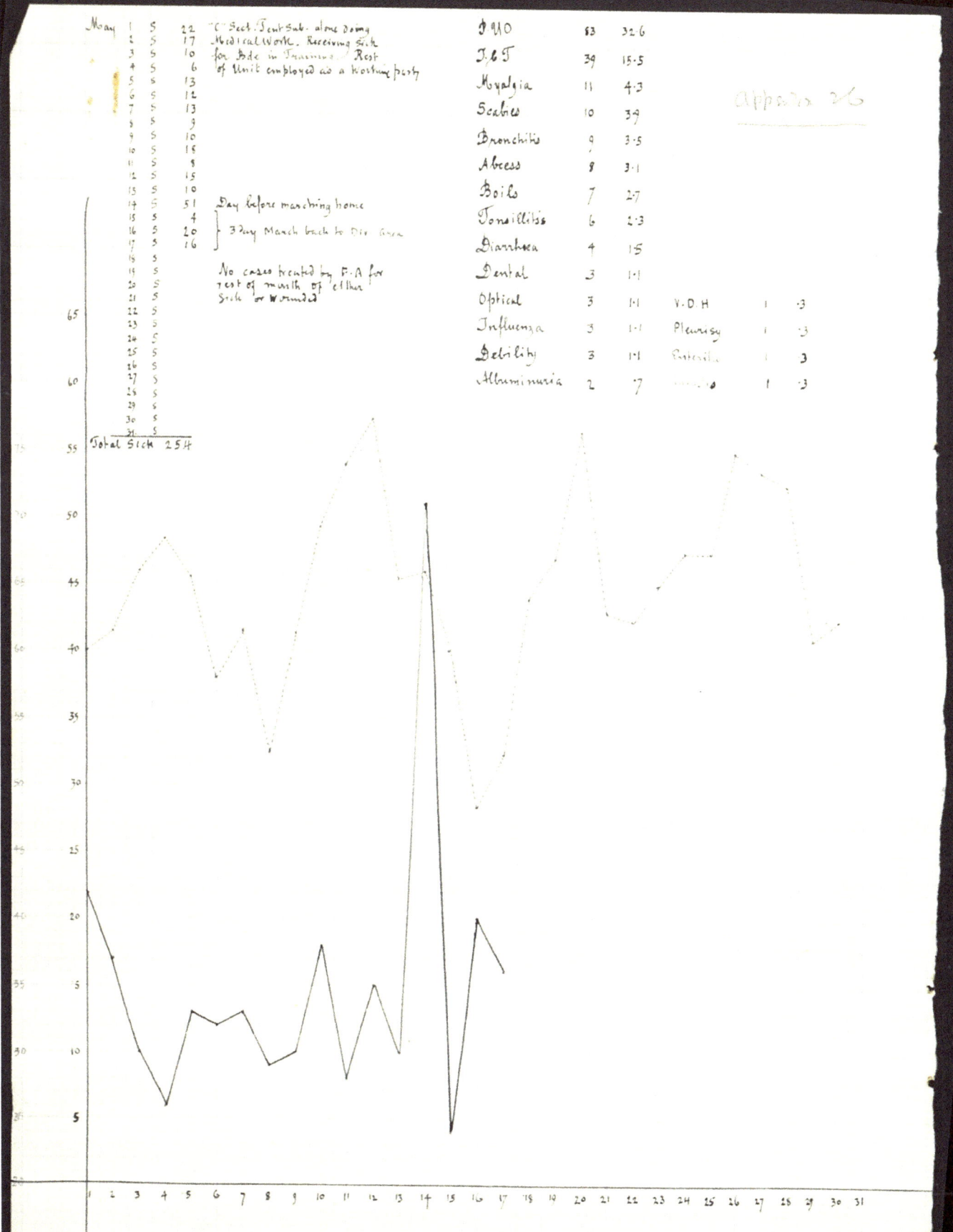

May			
1	S	22	"C" Sect. Tent Sub. alone doing
2	S	17	Medical Work. Receiving Sick
3	S	10	for Bde in Trammes. Rest
4	S	6	of Unit employed as a Working party
5	S	13	
6	S	12	
7	S	13	
8	S	9	
9	S	10	
10	S	15	
11	S	8	
12	S	15	
13	S	10	
14	S	51	Day before marching home
15	S	4	
16	S	20	} 3 Day March back to Div Area
17	S	16	
18	S		
19	S		No cases treated by F.A for
20	S		rest of month of either
21	S		Sick or Wounded
22	S		
23	S		
24	S		
25	S		
26	S		
27	S		
28	S		
29	S		
30	S		
31	S		

Total Sick 254

P.U.O	83	32.6
I.C.T	39	15.5
Myalgia	11	4.3
Scabies	10	3.9
Bronchitis	9	3.5
Abcess	8	3.1
Boils	7	2.7
Tonsillitis	6	2.3
Diarrhoea	4	1.5
Dental	3	1.1
Optical	3	1.1
Influenza	3	1.1
Debility	3	1.1
Albuminuria	2	.7

V.D.H	1	.3
Pleurisy	1	.3
Enteritis	1	.3
	1	.3

Appdx 26

24

June 1917

Confidential

140/230

War Diary.

Vol 14

140th Field Ambulance

R.A.M.C.

COMMITTEE FOR THE
MEDICAL HISTORY OF THE WAR
Date — 7 AUG. 1917

From 1/6/17 to 30/6/17

Army Form C. 2118

WAR DIARY
or
INTELLIGENCE SUMMARY

(Erase heading not required.)

130th Field Amb

Place	Date	Hour	Summary of Events and Information	Remarks and references to Appendices

Army Form C. 2118

WAR DIARY
or
INTELLIGENCE SUMMARY
(Erase heading not required.)

Place	Date	Hour	Summary of Events and Information	Remarks and references to Appendices
LA CLYTTE Rd M.O.S.	Jun 7	4am to 6	A steady stream of wounded which were officially dealt with by M.O. staff	
		6am		
		6.30	Edn. staff at there proper posts as detailed in my circulated arrangements. Wounded now arriving in continuous stream including prisoners of war.	
		10 am	A.D.M.S. visited M.D.S.	
		12.30	Surgeon MACPHERSON from G.H.Q. made thorough inspection of complete arrangements in large dining marquee. Dressings & dressing	
		2 h	Rations for 200 served in without hitch	
			Rations for further 3500	
		3 h	Rations for further 200	
		5 h		
		6 h	Total of 58 wounded made up for freight train on narrow gauge. Since that accommodation for more wounded had efficient horse service reached the mattresses. Wounded have been accommodated but continuous stream of wounded Jeept (sun) at 2 P.m. 104°F So the men refused by him light somewhat	
	Jun 8	10 -	A stop All wounded evacuated. Small parties known contained to assist. So the period of 36 hours from commencing zero 1363 wounded and about 50 sick were evacuated - 45 665 hot dinners were served. P.S.K. refreshments were provided by Y Men	

Instructions regarding War Diaries and Intelligence Summaries are contained in F. S. Regs., Part II. and the Staff Manual respectively. Title Pages will be prepared in manuscript.

WAR DIARY
or
INTELLIGENCE SUMMARY

(Erase heading not required.)

Army Form C. 2118

(3)

140th Field Ambulance.

Place	Date 1917	Hour	Summary of Events and Information	Remarks and references to Appendices
[illegible]	June 8	6 am	I handed over command to Major S. G. McALLUM. J R.	
[illegible]	[illegible] 8 D		I arrived last night (7/6/17) but took over formally to day checking equipment etc. Only a few minor deficiencies, & one or two articles unserviceable to be replaced. During the night a considerable number of wounded - slight - & some stretcher cases arrived. About 35 arrived during the day. Sgt [illegible] back from ADS with 30 bearers. Went over Hospital & familiarised myself with arrangements.	
Do.	" 9th		About 30 wounded last night. Kept coming in small numbers during day, also some sick. This forenoon Maj. Gen. Lawford C.B. G.O.C. 41st Div. called, stated that the evacuation of wounded was most satisfactory. Evac. of light wounded continue by Lorries	[illegible]
Do.	" 10th		DADMS X Corps called, stated that Lorries would be discontinued, Evacuation by our own Cars & M.A.C. Has been very hot, cooler today.	[illegible]
Do.	" 11th		All Transport & Motor Amb. returned from A.D.S. (taken by 138 Field Amb.). Orders received for our Amb. to take in all sick & wounded passed down from Voormezeele (the A.D.S.) a Bearer Subdivision & certain of our Motor Amb. to report at Voormezeele tomorrow.	[illegible]
"	" 12th		Capt. Davies & bearer Subdivision left for duty at Voormezeele with 138 F. Amb. They are collecting from R.A.P. to A.D.S. This Ambulance is now conducting M.D.S. for all wounded, & also a D.R.S. for Divisional sick (up to 200) but there are considerable numbers of sick from other Divisions. Sick & wounded continue to arrive during day & night at about 50-60 a day. Capt. Butler reported for duty from Havre. Lts. Hale & Nott Med. Officers in U.S. army joined for duty & instruction	[illegible]
"	13th		Quite a number of cases arrived (wounded) during last night & this forenoon. Sent Capt. Butler & 50 men under orders DDMS to clear up neighbourhood of Dickebusch Lake. DDMS X Corps called, & ordered by him to take over certain area stores, tents, stretchers etc.	[illegible]

1875 Wt. W593/826 1,000,000 4/15 J.B.C. & A. A.D.S.S./Forms/C. 2118.

Army Form C. 2118

WAR DIARY
or
INTELLIGENCE SUMMARY
(Erase heading not required.)

1st Ft [Pult?]

Place	Date	Hour	Summary of Events and Information	Remarks and references to Appendices
M.D.S. La Clytte Rd M & A & B	1917 June 14th	7.30pm	Attack of H.Ns 44 Division. 138th A.D. conducting A.D.S. at Voormezeele. This Ambulance acted as M.D.S. & D.R.S. (up to 200 cases in the Parties). 70 wounded received by trainfrt. S.A.Bus & 8 lorries called in evening to say M.A.C. were over, satisfactorily. Conference of C.Os at Abuis. Capt Davies v 50 & Brake Subdivision returned from 138th 9 Ind D. Reservillon on our personel.	MW [?]
	15th		Went carefully over all cases on M.F.S & B.N.S. to sort out accumulation also post of & number of cars. R.T.D to F.S. See Reinforcement Camp Butch reinforced & kind on Dossing totaly, returned. Stoke does this was opened bathing etc. Most fruits of sptd. moved by D.Dmt to return Brazerbabaheim to 138 2nd [Inde?] Infaby. All itself called resent 2nd [scheme?] Camp. Considerable number of sick recovered	[?]
	18th		Heavy thunderstorm & green them wither much cooler.	[?]
	19th		Sent up Capt Davidson v Lt Nutt (U.S.M.C.) for duty at A.D.S. Voormezeele with 138 2 Ind.	[?]
	21st		Arrival of Bathoff Board. O.C. inspection of men, men's clothing on a bad state. Some shelling of Reinmghilst.	[?]
	22nd			
	23rd		Order received that Lt./o.m. Whitney goes for duty to 14 General Hosp. Chas named Horse transport with A.D. Regt my sent inspection of Horses Transport. He former quite satisfactory on the whole, but harness inefficient well kept. Sent Capt Butler to relieve Capt Saunderson at Voormezeele A.D.S. Lt/v D.M. Whitney left for 14 General Hosp. Capt Davies to 15th H. Hands Regt for temporary duty	[?]
	24th			

Instructions regarding War Diaries and Intelligence Summaries are contained in F. S. Regs., Part II. and the Staff Manual respectively. Title Pages will be prepared in manuscript.

WAR DIARY
or
INTELLIGENCE SUMMARY
(Erase heading not required.)

Army Form C. 2118

(5)

140th Field Ambulance

Place	Date 1917	Hour	Summary of Events and Information	Remarks and references to Appendices
M.D.S. & D.R.S. La Clytte 28 N.6.A.8.8	June 25th		Shorthanded in officers, so I saw the morning sick over 100. Later in day Capt Butler came down from Voormezeele for duty here. Operation orders received from A.D.M.S. re move on the 30th to new area. We march with 124 Bgde. Sent Capt Harrison on to new area with some personnel to take over, Capt Harrison returned same evening. D.A.D.M.S. Corps, called. Steady flow of sick & wounded, one man died in D.R.S. from Epilepsy	[illegible]
"	26th		Inspected a number of so called N.Y.D.N. most of them have quite recovered & have been returned to duty. The D.D.M.S. X Corps called. Lt Col Williamson who is taking over this camp (47th Division) called & went over camp, & got some detail re stores to be handed [illegible]	[illegible]
"	27th		A.D.M.S. called, we are now to evacuate to Bailleul C.C.S. In our new area have to take over clearing of evac. of 122 Bgde. Issued the necessary orders.	
"	28th		A.D.M.S. heard here. Capt Harrison went on to new billets, [illegible] sick from 122nd Bgde, with necessary personnel, dressings etc. All our Bearer Sub-divisions returned from 138 F. Amb. also the Motor Amb. Sorted out all the patients [illegible] R.T.D. or to go to 139 F. Amb. who take on the 29th [illegible] not sufficiently recovered for duty. In afternoon had to send up two [illegible] to get some cases at Voormezeele	[illegible]
Camp X 16 D.9.9	30th		4th Lond. Field Amb. arrived 9.0 a.m. Handed over during forenoon. Received receipts for area, Corps. & R.E. [illegible] stores. Cleared out all patients from D.R.S., left some of 47th Div. to the [illegible] at [illegible] Left our billets 6.45 pm. marched with 124 Brigade, via Kemmel, Westoutre, Berthen to camp at X 16 D.9.9 on Bailleul - Meteren road. Arrived midnight. Men & horses marched well. Had to leave Roan horse behind (temporarily) as it was lame. Reported arrival to A.D.M.S. & 124th Bgde. Men in camp. Starting a D.R.S. in this camp for 50 patients. The surplus above this to go to 139 Field Amb. Bgde. H.Q. at Meteren.	

[illegible]
O.C. 140th F. Amb.

1875 Wt. W593/826 1,000,000 4/15 J.B.C. & A. A.D.S.S./Forms/C. 2118.

No. 15

Confidential
War Diary
140th Field Ambulance
R.A.M.C.

From 1st July 1917
To 31st July 1917

WAR DIARY
or
INTELLIGENCE SUMMARY

(Erase heading not required.)

Army Form C. 2118

Vol. XI R.A.M.C.

14th Field Ambulance

Place	Date	Hour	Summary of Events and Information	Remarks and references to Appendices
Camp X at X16.D.8.8 Sheet 27B S.W.	July 1917 1st		Arrived just after 12.0 a.m. put up tents, mortmen in brazier, B.H.Q at Metern, Div H.Q Berthen. Arrangements made for collecting & evacuating sick & 124 v 122 Regts. B.W. Rect for 50 patients - We opened their own.	AMW
	2nd		for men, whilst we draw 10 extra tents to evacuate sick to Bailleul. Sent 6 Bgr cases to Hazebrouck. Lines put up. 10 tents detailed Capt Booth to collect 6 ach of 122 Rgt, St Sylvestre (U.S.A) for 124th Bgd. Planned general scheme of training for afternoon, afternoon for men's recreation. Bailleul & Hazebrouck heavily bombed by Hostile planes.	AMW
		10 pm		
	4th		Training started. D.A.D.M.S visited. Very hot.	AMW
	6th		Had informally this Amb. will run M.D.S for seriously wounded in next offensive at the La Clytte Rd Camp. Started training every afternoon.	AMW
	7th		A.D.M.S & officers visited district to obtain views. Went up to Brandhoek for suggestions re M.D.S Beware wounded. Then on to La Clytte Rd Camp, saw O.C. there 128 C.C. Williamson. Talked over suggested changes to readings & road attraction of Magan tonight. My own take preparation for 500 seriously wounded in the camp. Capt Rowtherd returned from leave.	AMW
	8th		Held over ambulance for O.C., twenty ambulances to run at Bret. Brig Recy. The Sgt Maj, (Pilgrim) went on leave. Observed some sound with Capt. Bentsley & Bowden.	AMW
	9th		This M.D.S. in most effective.	AMW
			Went to Remy for Conference dental treatment. Capt Lawes went on local capt - Harrison rehened him at Regt.	AMW
	11th		Released from duties.	
	12th		2 N.C.Os 30 men to La Clytte Camp Shelf Zoned, G.O. in work of construction. Capt Rowland went up to L'hotel Camp, observed some sharpnel shell bursting in water Co of chlorine + carbolic.	
	13th		Much bombing of Bailleul had rapid & Poelka, P.Ss. money, no casualty. Observed bombarding of Proven & Poperinghe, B.E.F (hostile) nightful. Tomorrow about inspection off.	AMW

Army Form C. 2118

WAR DIARY
or
INTELLIGENCE SUMMARY 140th Field Ambulance
(Erase heading not required.)

Instructions regarding War Diaries and Intelligence Summaries are contained in F.S. Regs., Part II. and the Staff Manual respectively. Title Pages will be prepared in manuscript.

Place	Date 1917 July	Hour	Summary of Events and Information	Remarks and references to Appendices
Camps at X.16.2.88	14th		G.O.C. 41st Div. visited unit at Amb. 9.30 a.m. Inspected men, Horses, Horse Transport, Amb. was drawn up in sections, & in saluting line. General expressed his approval. Conference at Head of Amb. C.O.'s discussed coming Divisional & O.C.'s Garden Party afternoon. Arranged for Divisional Football Tournament competition. C.O.'s Garden Party as a unit.	4pm
do	16th		To Chafaux M.D.S. (La Clytte Rd.) enquired about palliasses, stretchers etc, inspect after this O.C. & then has returned several things to Ordnance. Ambulance losses heavy. Rain for two football finals 3rd & 2nd & 2.	4pm
do	17th		Ambulance from Head — 20 Middlesex Regt. 1 good to O. for Divisional Prize. Ordered in afternoon that we move tomorrow to Westoutre area, move to be complete by noon. The march 7.45 a.m. Packs up in evening.	4pm
Hop	18th		Heavy rain last night — Ambulance moved 7.45 a.m. Road march via Berthen, Westoutre to Conquerors Camp near Hokstem (corner Westoutre) arriving held-area — 10.45am. Drew 10 tents from Area Stores (Westoutre) put up our huts ready to receive up to 50 patients. Lt. 7th R.C. Sydney & Largel met at Meteren Camp. Hurcombe has drawn unable to complete orders to move. Lt. Hale R.A.M.C. (U.S.) to 10th Queens as Temporary Capt. M.O. Ambulance team beat – Am. returner in the final for Divisional football prize 2 goals to O.	4pm
Conquerors Camp Westoutre				
do	19th		Sgt. Macy Pilgrim (R.9.M.R.) returned from Leave.	
do	20th		O.C.'s conference at A.D.M.S. Divisional H.Q.	
do	21st		O.C.'s conference at A.D.M.S. Divisional H.Q. 20 Divisional Shelter & blankets, sketches & allowed at 2 M.D.S. We noted All Junior Officers attended A.D.M.S. conference at 138 Field Amb. Much arrangement for coming Divisional Advance described to them.	
do	23rd		Orders from A.D.M.S. Sent Capt. Davies to temp M.O. 15/H Hants & Capt. Harrison to 8/15, 12/H Surrey, the latter was returned 9 p.m. could not be looked out as Capt. Davies ordered to join the Regiment in the dark. Rev. MacParrey joined Ambulance	4pm

1875 Wt. W593/326 1,000,000 4/15 J.B.C. & A. A.D.S.S./Forms/C. 2118.

Army Form C. 2118

WAR DIARY
or
INTELLIGENCE SUMMARY
(Erase heading not required.)

1/1 O/R Field Ambulance

Place	Date	Hour	Summary of Events and Information	Remarks and references to Appendices
Longueau Camp	1917 July 24th		Capt Davies left for 15th Hamps temp duty to relieve Capt Harrison. This officer (Harrison) had to come into H of E. Temp 102°. Orders received. Brigade to Chipawa Camp America. Both above level-V	Appx
	25.		Shower bath. R of Egypt. Removed about 50 patients W.T.A.S. at Boeschepe. Heavy rain in field. Unit moved to Chipawa Camp via Dickiebusch.	
Chipawa Camp La Clytte	26.	11.30 am	to Locken 9 bars. Shoes camp. Lt. Morgan visiting arrangements for running this as A.D.S. 9 stores etc. Wounded. Remained as unwounded camb. The Rev. M. Gay - Church Service, Junior as	Appx
	27.		a busy member of H of R from this unit. Sunday & onwards. Reluctant received (Rev) Harrison to day held as a temp duty. C.O. Conference at 2 Find officer discussed all points. Wound arrangement as follows.	
			B.C.N. 3rd London Div. walking wounded Dick... and H.Q. at Ypstrasse. Capt Harrison issued as O every med. from 2.5.G. arrived by a Fact (overlooking) expected in case of enemy attack. It was a superimposed arrangement so having 2 being. wounded to ... Post M. Stretcher. Ironside fully mounted fronts. M.G... But. Other small 5 stores at this. M.P.K. Jones Ref. Aide in Saloons W.R.L below under the shoes of ... Post that what with...	
			line assisting A.M.B.S. of R.B.S. ahead of one. 250 or 400, evidently they have not returned yet. Continued advance investigation both and supply of Evacuation to the attack. N.Z.H.D. & Bays W.R.L in	Appx
	28.		night.	
	29.	2.30 am	Gas alarm after 1.30 probably some shelling Gas fume shells. Include the new gas. Breast wind Lachrymery Nasal irrit... also Iritt Lachrymery poisonous Can find with Cork R.C. Conference with no officers at H.Q. arrangements for Evac. Complete Eval. with the Rev. Phelan sort. B. Moran. St. John stretcher + hampri 6 G.O. 483. Can't Ruffle from ... as my opinion for Joves Salva 80 Parade here. Completed work of wl. stretcher ... ... stretcher each parade bearer.	Appx

from 1.30 to 2.30

WAR DIARY
or
INTELLIGENCE SUMMARY

Army Form C. 2118

140 Field Amb.

Place	Date	Hour	Summary of Events and Information	Remarks and references to Appendices
Chippawa Camp de Clytte Rd	1917 July 30th	6.30 am	Two bearer subdivs, H. Trans for 1 M. Amb. & ADS at Voormezeele. O.C. 140 M.A.C. called & arranged about necessary cars. Considerable number of slightly wounded arriving. G.O.C. Lt. Malborn wounded Busseboom (Dressing Station). At 9.30 pm he could not get to see O.C. 1/London F.A. Malborn wounded sent message he was ready to evacuate, so sent till he came till midnight but afterwards sent message all right wounds mine. Considerable number of gassed cases, several requiring blanketing & oxygen. M.S.A. Trans Corps reld cast 3 OC 11th M.A.C. now had 10 cars, & have 20 at 8 a.m. tomorrow.	Apps
"	31st		2 day. Zero hour 3.50 am. From midnight to 6 am. 4 & one. all evac & await'd. C. Amb't. & b.t. finden Motor halted, meantime used Hosp. 38th Inf Corps hospital foreman. Sug. Jon. Macpherson about 2 form hant-arose Stons Six Corps also visited.	
		6 pm	Steady flow of wounded & gassed coming to Walker Road, one especially bad, & came oxygen with good about. Aprox - 12.1st. of War.	Amb
		6.30 pm	197 all ranks since midday had, evacuations running smoothly.	
		thro' night	Very few cases come in since 6.30 those all been evac'd, two even evac'd even since. Bearers parties. Offensive thus has been no great difficulty in evacuating, this afternoon. Eldin and that in conducting M.B.S. & bearers & bringing to a large number of stretcher bearers are required for carrying from front to link.	Amb

Stuart My Allan
Lt Col RAMC
O.C. 140 F Amb.

Aug 1917

27 No 16

140/241/38

Confidential

From DDMS

140 Field Ambulance

R.A.M.C.

To:—

3rd Army Hospital

COMMITTEE FOR THE
MEDICAL HISTORY OF THE WAR
Date −5 NOV.1917

140 Field Ambulance.
War Diary.
August, 1917.

Army Form C. 2118

WAR DIARY
or
INTELLIGENCE SUMMARY

(Erase heading not required.)

Vol. XVI

140th Field Amb.

Instructions regarding War Diaries and Intelligence Summaries are contained in F.S. Regs., Part II. and the Staff Manual respectively. Title Pages will be prepared in manuscript.

Place	Date	Hour	Summary of Events and Information	Remarks and references to Appendices
Chippewa M.D.S. La Hytte Rd	1911 August 1		Heavy rain during night. Wounded cases received since [illegible] to 6 a.m. = 27 all ranks. Bomb. B.A.m 6-12 noon. 1 officer V.Q.D.R. [illegible] II Corps [illegible], also [illegible] 47th Div. Also 7th [illegible] Corps Commander (Gen T.H. Morland M.C.B. etc.)	[illegible] Weather
		7 pm	Orders from A.D.M.S. to send Officer to report at [illegible] 3 & L. St Stratton. [illegible] Capt. Spin 5/L Shelters to D.O.C. 134 (complete) [illegible] [illegible] [illegible] in order that 7th Halc A.M.C. W.S. will be permanently attached to Dr. P.W. Currys (Queens) [illegible]	
	2nd		[illegible] considerable number of wounded in afternoon. Extract from 2nd Army General [illegible] Routine Orders [illegible] suggests shelter to Rd Amb as dressing station, reported later. R Amb [illegible] also R Amb 147 Brig. Walked wounded [illegible] also resident Sussex Rgs of wounded.	June 2 [illegible]
	3rd	6.30 pm	[illegible] in evening. Orders from [illegible] [illegible] that [illegible] have [illegible] of every [illegible]. [illegible] [illegible] [illegible]. Staff mounted all our [illegible] & Ambulances to 3 car Hosp.	
	4th	6 am	[illegible] [illegible] [illegible] [illegible] at Hay [illegible] [illegible] actions etc. Large number of sick in [illegible] [illegible] sent by Amy = 487 including 23 Officers + 23 P.O. War Pkmed that 2 Dras Ambulances have been [illegible] at Spoil Bank Shelters S.P. Huy Yprs Loos & one in [illegible] lay [illegible] (will be [illegible]) 41 evacuated MMc MDS, 14 MO etc.	
	5th		41 [illegible] [illegible] [illegible] [illegible] know to take the [illegible] [illegible] Capt D.B. MacLachlan reported for Duty from Army for serving in M[illegible] in France. Lt. Harrison reported from 71st Field Amb. Two marquees [illegible] by 71 Field Amb. On [illegible] of Williams. Evacuated 7/Fd Hass return 260 to M.D.S. with 1st R.M.	
	6th		Ambulance now conducting M.D.S. for all wounded also Hospital to retain up to 300 sick. Much necessary [illegible] [illegible] [illegible] P Sbau Subdu. Wounded 6 Relay horses [illegible] Steady stream of sick [illegible] all day. Pt Johnson [illegible] this Amb wounded v 2 killed	[illegible]

WAR DIARY or INTELLIGENCE SUMMARY

Army Form C. 2118

160 Field Amb. (2)

Place	Date	Hour	Summary of Events and Information	Remarks and references to Appendices
Chippawa Miss La Clytte Rd.	August 7th		Large number of morning sick, considerable number of Wounded Officers called, no that to handing over of short notice. O.C. 139 F. Amb. expressed satisfaction of good work done by Sgt Beck. Q.M. M.T. also Cpl Piper R.A.M.C.	HW
"	8th		Instructed to have 100 cases (sick) to go to Special C.C.S. when we move to the Reft on our troops Lt Harrison posted to our Amb from 6th Amb. Began checking and other stores. Serving Brunt(?) & filling in Field Med. Cards. Drew up a set of instructions	HW
	10th		Lt Harvey U.S. Army Med Corps joined for duty	HW
	11th		Heavy bombing early this morning by hostile Aeroplanes. D.C.O's Conference at 8 Aus	HW
	12th		Inspected details about more etc. Orders re move 14/15th	HW
	13th		Lt Strothers back to Amb. Futine Adv	
			to 136 F.A. arranged for loan of 2 G.S. wagon. Heavy 10 tents to our new area. Then went out to see out who killed near Flats.	
			In evening orders arrived to have our complete section ready for detached duty. Detached B Sect. with Capt Rowland Woodlark & Lt Harrison	HW
	14th		Handing over to 133 F.A. 35th Div. Evacuated all unfit sick returned to duty about 50 men left Hosp. elsew of our Division. Sent on Capt Davidson & 2 sections to our new camp at W.S. C.3.Q. (Near Flats). Capt. Harrison to S. Survey & return Capt. Herdman. Handed our all and other stores.	
W.S.C.3.Q. (Flete Shute Rd)	15th		B section under Capt. Rowland was left for Woodlark & crew Lt Strothers left Amb. for Base Sel. Stretcher party arrived with wounded, near Flete at 11.am. Lebels up & ready to accommodate to 50 patients. Men in bivvie. We applied to 122 Bde at present	HW
	16th		ADMS visited	HW

Army Form C. 2118

WAR DIARY
or
INTELLIGENCE SUMMARY
(Erase heading not required.)

140 Field Amb. (3)

Place	Date	Hour	Summary of Events and Information	Remarks and references to Appendices
Camp W.6.C.3.9 (Hebu sheet 27)	August 1917 18th		Three years since landed in France with refined B.E.F. aShd called. In evening hostile aeroplane bombed heavily in neighbourhood of camp. One bomb in camp with over 80 casualties. Sent Capt Davidson with available Ambulances.	JHM
"	19"		Orders received march tomorrow with 122 Regt. at 7 a.m. to form near Nova Rava in dem from ADnd 2 march. Arranged for march etc.	
"	20"		Capt Davidson went on leave. 2 a.m. Ambulance marched 7 a.m. via Hondeghem. S.lapeler to form at N.30 about 1/2 kilom E. of E. of Houck. (Orders reads about 4 kilom S.E. of Rovinchove. distance about 12 miles arrived about 1pm Men in barns. Sent car round for as en to 4 hours re evac. b 7 pm. Hop. St Omer. orders for Brunions march arrived about 7 p.m. Recmmts evac b 7 pm. Hop. St Omer. orders for Brunions march arrived about 7 p.m. Column marched at 8.15 a.m. via St Omer, St Martins, Bouleghem, 15 La Wattine Gough	JHM
La Wattine (sheet 27 S.E.)	21"		Into small field. Went in advance for billets. Amb. arrived about 5:30 p.m. Men in barns all available pits of tins every morning - hulls from holes watered Queens H.Q. Sus. H. Q. at Wizernes. 1 h.2" B.H.Q. at Boisdog Kam. Could accommodate with tents teams up to 70. Arranged for collecting of sick. Brigade convalescents scattered. To C.O's conference at -Wnd ADnd selected third field on P.B. men. To arrange the tents on the common or had send some of the detail. Parade this in field W.22.d.	JHM
80	22"			JHM
80	23"		for Interpreter orders arrived rather for C.m.C's inspection. tom arrive (W. Nev.), practiced	JHM
80	24"		Men left for C.M.C's inspection at 7 a.m. send 2 wagon v b o A.R. The B.A rues spread some detail at 9:30 a.m. Sir Douglas Haig inspected 11 a.m. weather showery. Everything went well. OT& well.	JHM

1875 Wt. W593/826 1,000,000 4/15 J.B.C. & A. A.D.S.S./Forms/C. 2118.

Army Form C. 2118

WAR DIARY
or
INTELLIGENCE SUMMARY

140th Field Ambulance

(Erase heading not required.)

Place	Date 1917	Hour	Summary of Events and Information	Remarks and references to Appendices
La Mattine (Sheet 27, S.E.)	August 25th		Interpreter not yet arrived. 6.0 a.m. unable to move tents yet. Weather very strong.	
	27th		Effected an exchange of 4 men with B. Section. Still most of the men had all over their hay. Capt. Gordon Watson Consult: Surgeon 2nd Army gave a demonstration on newly prepared Zinc Iodine for local staph strands along with the Thomas M/o Astay visited patient & wound. Afterwards arrived & stated he could move onto the Common, but weather at present unfavorable.	M/o
	29th		Capt. MacLachlan arrived from Westoutre (B. Section) in July, no officer need report for duty.	
	30th		Completed first series of training. Men have had Physical, Stretcher & Squad drill. Also Route march in forenoon, afternoon they have been Rd-Vessup-ment information for mechanical purposes, and one man to Parson Institute under orders of A.D.M.S – Inspected rabbits from dog bite.	
	31st		Ten R.B. men arrived for duty all lotus from Bailleul & Corner Sent Away 10 men to A.Sc. H.Q. 65 Heavy A.Brand 41st Div. MD0 50 of 31st	M/o

J.M. Allen
Lt Col RAMC
Oc 140 F.A.

War Diary
of
140 Field Ambulance
for
September 1917

Vol 7

Army Form C. 2118

WAR DIARY
or
INTELLIGENCE SUMMARY
Vol XVII
140 Field Ambulance

(Erase heading not required.)

Place	Date	Hour	Summary of Events and Information	Remarks and references to Appendices
La Wattine	1917 September 1st		In same billets. A.D.M.S. conference of C.O.s at Wizerne, discussed certain administrative & other points. Capt. Davidson returned from leave.	Appx
"	2nd		Weather rather finer. So moved small tents up to the Common Fort - all cornered. Paid advance. Interviewed all the P.B. men, not very hopeful regarding H.T. duties. The divisional Cross country run held near La Fosse Farm, and although limb entered a team, the first place in run was won by R.A.M.C. men (138 Field Amb.), over 300 competitors. Our team finished 5th. Number of aeroplanes - hostile - over at night. 5 P.B. men from Regt. to A.D.M.S. Board.	Appx
"	3rd		Sent men for P.B. to St Omer. R.T.O. wired me directed from Div. (G) to bring them back & all 60. reporting to A.D.M.S. Capt Davidson gave evidence in F.G. Court martial	Appx
"	5th		German taken Riga. Orders from A.D.M.S. 9pm. to send Capt Davies, 2 N.C.O.s & 30 men (fly hus) to area of Ridge Wood as working party on the 6th. L'bus to send on the 6th. 1 Limber, 1 G.S. Wagon, 1 Watercart. To Walton Capel, Jr Ridge Wood area.	Appx
"	6th		The three was one left of Walton Capel. Go up tomorrow with C.R.E. & S.A. Fmd to see A.D.S. the men the tents.	Appx
"	7th		Left Wizernes with S.A Fmd 5.30 a.m. B ds Clytte on with C.R.E. to near Lock Wood, our new A.D.S. made suggestions re arrangement back from Larch Wood to Pedebanden Rd. etc, then on to Canada St. an A.B.D.and at Collect Post, which is at present being modified. Then to Hedge St. which has still two dug out. S A Fmd M.O.R. went on to R.A.P. (Chin Amb, is to near the A.D.S.) Returned to Larch Wood & thence vis track to Lock Wood (A.D.S.) & Voormezeele & to a great deal of work & trolley line being constructed), thence for evacuation of wounded. Capt Davidson on board at Westoutre, at forming of some tents. Capt Doyle arrived to study from with the Ambulance.	Appx

Army Form C. 2118

WAR DIARY
or
INTELLIGENCE SUMMARY
(Erase heading not required.)

Instructions regarding War Diaries and Intelligence Summaries are contained in F.S. Regs., Part II. and the Staff Manual respectively. Title Pages will be prepared in manuscript.

140 Field Amb.

(2)

Place	Date	Hour	Summary of Events and Information	Remarks and references to Appendices
La Wattine	1917 Sept.	8th	Attend conference. Heard of orders re coming offensive.	MM
"		11th	Attend conference. Went over orders for offensive. Brig. & other M.O.s present.	MM
"		13th	Went in advance to Westoutre. Was about half time at Voormezeele it 7.15 go over some of the ground. Called at A.D.M.S office on way back. D.D.M.S also the G.O.C inspecting the work at Hedge St.	MM
Wallon Cappelle	14th		Ambulance marched from Wattine to Wallon Cappelle area, Flêtre. Preceded to Voormezeele, saw O.C. 134 F.A. at present there & got full particulars regarding material the take over at different posts, personnel etc. On to Lock 8 which will form our A.D.S. Saw accommodation etc. Then down to Voormezeele hose lines. Voormezeele rather unhealthy for horse standing as they shell through. Telephone connects Lock 8, Larch Wood (Collect Post) & A.D.S. would have preferred it at Voormezeele.	MM
Flêtre - Nieppe Forest	15th		Ambs. in ach'd Wallon Cappelle to Mt. Flêtre. I called at A.D.M.S near Reninghelst.	MM
Veerstraat	16th		Then went down to car Amb. Amb. car marched 2.30 to how lines at Veerstraat, troops journey 1 hour rest at Westoutre.	MM
"		17th	Called for Capts. Davidson, Butler & Doyle & personnel of 44. Took over "Lock 8" as Adv. D.S. Left Capt. Butler incharge with 14 men, on to Larch Wood (Collect Post) Capt. Davidson & 15 men to take over. Capt. Doyle & 14 men to Canada St. Adv. D.P. to take over. Hedge St. not yet complete. Gave my instructions briefly & actually take over. To A.D.M.S for conference at 3 p.m. Jo Jenny Choppy 39 A.Buy R.F.A. stopped tornies to evacuate walking wounded. Sent arrangements for distribution of equip. etc to the different posts.	MM

WAR DIARY
INTELLIGENCE SUMMARY

14 O Field Ambulance

Army Form C. 2118

Remarks and references to Appendices: 3/

Place	Date/Hour	Summary of Events and Information	Remarks
Voormazeele	18th Sept	Major & Lt. Harvey on duty through each, as neither B Sect. nor Working party (80) had proved as any distinctly short handed. Steady flow of wounded during the night. Adms. called round this eve, told him my General actions, that I proposed staying at Voormazeele as my services were more urgent there. Adms. sent up 300 stretchers, drew 150 more from the DADs at Brecchaepe, & 400 Blankets from O.C. 139 J.A. The greatest part of the equipment for the B.A.Ps & other posts along with the rations for personnel packed & sent up by Trollies - mule drawn - to the different posts. B. section from Weston to the working party from Ridge Wood, & rest up later in the day, so sent up reinforcements to the different posts with some more equipment. Many approx 153 wounded & many sick seen.	
"	19th	Steady flow of wounded, majority not of our Division, to be congested at times but was still to deal with the evacuations by our Amb., & Horse Transport Lorries. Personally transport arrived from 138. Personnel of 138 B (bearers), some further equip. & Nursing S- Sent up to ... Dumley to Canada St. Dob. C.P. The eqpt for RAPs & CPs now complete as handed over in Armd orders. Capt Lowder & two other officers from 138-39 arrived & proceeded to Larch Wood	
	6.30 pm	Capt Bosse & personnel from 139 D (also transport) arrived. Sent them on to their respective posts under Capt Bosse also the rations for the different posts. Capt Rowland reports everything satisfactory at Trolley 8.	
	8 pm	All personnel & transport now in place. Steady flow of sick & wounded all day approx all numbers flatter being treated. 985.	

AMG

Army Form C. 2118

WAR DIARY
or
INTELLIGENCE SUMMARY
(Erase heading not required.)

140 Field Amb.

Place	Date	Hour	Summary of Events and Information	Remarks and references to Appendices
Poperinghe	Sept 19 1917		(Continued) There has never been any blocking all wounded got away by 11.0.05. Transport. Field Cards issued. Nearly all three lorries got off about 9 pm one was sent to Sec. 8 & 2 about midnight – were ordered up to the stand near Jackson's Dump on the Mr Brandon Noten road. The one driver knew his way gave the officers proceeding to their posts. Interviewed them & submitted what transport there was personally. Equipment, satisfaction was expressed. No untoward occurrence. The Moten Rail was discussed with Capt Lawder of Jack Wood section. He ask'd for 6 motor Amb at by at Jacksons Dump. Twenty 8 pdr subsection & Vallies working. Zero. Capt Chesney the 3 Reser Sub/n, of 139 F. Amb. Conrad & 51 Capt Doyle, 8 tent Sub/n 6 Vallies under MO Questered under Capt Donaldson 3 Bearer Sub/n of this Amb (including about 10 from 139 F.A. brought up in number) Jack Wood Capt Saunder Sec. 3 with 3/others (U.S.A.N.Q.) 18 tent Sub/n, 18 Vallies, 30 S. Bearers. Locks & Capt Skerlund, Butter Haviour & 3 mt Sub/n 40 S. Bearers, 4 Vallies Voormezeele Myself, Capt Busse, Patterson & Henry, 1 tent Sub/n 16 S. Bearers. V.10 in Reserve (which was of course discharged last afternoon & should do!) With sick on hand at Count this Amb, is in our chief in first Sub/n.	
		Midnight	Orders issued to Lorries that this position, 4 6 motor Amb, to report to Capt Lawder at Jackson's Dump & each Sub to be returned by midnight. Capt Busse had not returned by midnight.	

J. Spellman

Army Form C. 2118

WAR DIARY
or
INTELLIGENCE SUMMARY
(Erase heading not required.)

140 Field Amb.

Place	Date Hour	Summary of Events and Information	Remarks and references to Appendices
Voormazeele	1917 September 20	About 3 a.m. Capt. Brose returned having got all his men to their destination. Heavy rain 1-6 a.m. Steady flees of wounded, some bad cases (all Divisions 39", 23"x11") also some gas. Bu. had care of beautiful haemorrhage, chloroform etc. Up all night again. Further wounded about 9 a.m. different Divisions, stretcher walking cases. The Congestion was great till about 11 a.m. Threatened to become one at times, all owing to passage full to overflow, many waiting outside, from about 9 a.m. was forced to send on all 39 Div. walking cases to the Brasserie owing to the Congestion, but at no time were we actually blocked, the evacuation by Horse Transport, lorries & Motor Amb. worked smoothly, Subs at this time unable many to number of cases to issue Field Med. Cards to all, I was also forced for same reason to send some on to R.B. Coll. without taking names. Many cases coming from Lock 8 — walking etc — who had been dressed, did not require dressing, came in & added to the Congestion, this was remedied. Capt. Samida called (in a car) early morning & stated he was not able to find any of the Motor Amb. at Jacksons dump, assured him they had been sent up according to arrangements. (16 M.A. by 20 min after Zero), also later after enquiry that some of the cars had returned with wounded, only they were chiefly 39 D Division, it was evident that a dressing station of this Division had used our cars freely, I spoke over to Capt. Louden, owing to telephonic break down Capt. Louden was unable to get into communication with me (on Lock 8). Agreed to send up more cars, explaining to his orderlies that if he so desired it he could have the use of every Motor Amb. He replied that, the Killis were practically useless from Larch Wood, & that there was a blockage at Larch Wood, that is had been made	57
		used the Corps Railway	

WAR DIARY or INTELLIGENCE SUMMARY

Army Form C. 2118

Instructions regarding War Diaries and Intelligence Summaries are contained in F.S. Regs., Part II. and the Staff Manual respectively. Title Pages will be prepared in manuscript.

140 Field Amb.

Place	Date	Hour	Summary of Events and Information	Remarks and references to Appendices
Voormezeele	1917 Sept 20	(Continued)	The DDMS called & went round the Dressing Station. 2 ABens called & told me of the Block at Larch Wood. 2 ABens called & told me of the Block at Larch Wood, assured him that 107 Amb. had been to Jackson's dump was overused with cap. & cars, that other cars had already been sent up. Evacuation of Lock 8, Voormezeele &c was going smoothly. A Jams called on his way back from Larch Wood, & told me of the Block there, & gave assured him that was who sent all afterwards that certainly some not there. I say by the 39 Div. that also that other with the new burying in been in consultation — Jackson's dump, also informed him that arrangements had been made for a time service of cars, that Horse Lines & why being sent up to aid in the evacuation with present time Amb. cars had been emptied at Voormezeele & returned direct to Larch Wood (except Abdomin- al, Chest, & cases not requiring fresh dressing, in which case the car was sent straight on to Chippawa). Another empty car sent to Larch Wood, in this way an ample full supply, on the whole 10 cars of the 9 A Bus as representing the DDMS was instructed to send all cars with all cases straight on to Chippawa, just so that no cars would call at Voormezeele either going or coming, provided but that this would not accelerate the car service in my opinion, as mixing with convoys & troops through the lengthened journey the cars would bring a serious chance of breaking between Voormezeele & Chippawa in addition to blocking the new dressing sta- tion Larch Wood Voormezeele. I accepted the idea. It was nothing at all likely the offensive about Voormezeele should rather than Larch Wood, as the latter was most important. I aimed up this all the time.	

Army Form C. 2118

WAR DIARY
or
INTELLIGENCE SUMMARY
(Erase heading not required.)

140 Field Amb.

Place	Date Hour	Summary of Events and Information	Remarks and references to Appendices
Voormezele	1917 September 20th (Cont)	By 3 p.m. Voormezele was practically empty. All cases had been evacuated, was the from this time onwards, as the cases were collected they were got away easily & quickly. The condition at Lock 8 were the same, only a small number of cases coming through, the majority of the walking wounded now seemed to make Lock 8 & came straight on to Voormezele. About 3.30 p.m. I phoned up to Larch Wood & received the report that the evacuations were well in hand, only about 30 cases remaining, that the service was satisfactory. Car service arranged as asked for by Capt Lauder. Steady stream of cases coming through, but no undue pressure. This continued till the end of the day. Approx. number of cases at Voormezele = 660, treated & dressed, this does not include sick treated on the spot, nor some wounded sent on whose names were not recorded. Orders from A.D.M.S. to change my H.Q. to Scott Wood Lock 8, did so, went round all the lines seeing the officers in charge, everything reported satisfactory at all the stations (Hedge St, Canada St, Larch Wood,) some repairs to the channings shortly, also stretcher remained, also Thomas splint remedied. Capt Lauder before MA Cars not required, enough to return them, the corps light railway now being used for evacuation. ¼ O.S. Bearers (Infantry) sent up by A.D.M.S. to assist in evacuation of forward areas. Capt Chesney to forward bearers Hedge S/7 has been wounded, Capt Parkhill from 139 will relieve. My H.Q. now Lock 8. — Wounded totals 83	20/9 5 M.A.Cars arrived 10 p.m. sent to Larch Wood.
"	21.81		

HMcCann

WAR DIARY
or
INTELLIGENCE SUMMARY.
(Erase heading not required.)

Army Form C. 2118.

140 Field Amb.

Place	Date Hour	Summary of Events and Information	Remarks and references to Appendices
Toul E	1919 Sept 22	Phone rang all night with acks & back word, apparent various changes planned in number of car & horses etc, all stations keeping the evacuations half in hand thus blocking the wounded here. In afternoon orders received per phone from officer that the Brewers will be relieved tonight 22/23. Certain machines received working order to Capt Lauder of the relief party him to communicate them & all concerned as he would be more easily able to do so. B.O. of 134 F.A. collision arranged with him his hours of relief viendles rendez [illegible] 7/2 136 F.A. [illegible] 8.30pm officers from Albert (Nov 31) arrived, received mine in correspondence with them with exception of pilot of officer to forward Bearers, arias of this convoy to be received till. I got in touch with O.C. relieving Amb. 134. — Shortly 136 F.A. personnel transport will be relieved by 3 p.m. 24". 139 F.A. by H.J. relieved by [illegible] 23rd then Amb. 134 to be 4 am. on 24". Capt Harries sent up to check work to help of necessary otherwise which he definitely [illegible] information on some points.	
"	23	Phone out of action Sept 14 am. Found we had been rendered River lost for L.8. Reported with M. H1 and any orders for relief went [illegible] Sent Capt Davies to Loneli Wood to report, as phone is broken, also Hosp.	[illegible]

A6945 Wt.W14422/M160 35,000 12/16 D. D. & L. Forms/C,2118/14.

WAR DIARY or INTELLIGENCE SUMMARY

Army Form C. 2118.

140 Light Amb.

9/

Place	Date	Hour	Summary of Events and Information	Remarks and references to Appendices
Locre	23 Sep 1917		(Cont) After some difficulty got into touch with OC 134 (Relieving Ambl) arranging with him for relief of the persons of 140 Off through Forward Bearer & Capt Stauden. Also sent orders then films in the afternoon	
		4.30 pm	Issued orders reference above. Heard that relief of 138 & 139 was delayed owing to their not getting their orders early enough. Their orders were issued by me directly I got the actual orders (8.30 previous night) a warning order having been previously sent out. Learnt that the light wounded sent by Cotes Railway from Lanch World had been taken to Remy siding instead of La Clytte as directed by Capt Stauden. Handed over took 8. Got a receipt from OC 187 BM. RD. (for signal officer)	Anne
Voormezeele		7.60	Moved to Voormezeele. Reported to Astrend at 10 pm, as situation of relief Capt Rowland (OC Voormezeele outposts told me that all personnel of Voormezeele of 138 & 139 have passed through Voormezeele, that the relief of them is complete. Parties from 138 X.O. have gone up to complete relief of 140 2.A Forward Bearer Officers. The Infantl. S. Bearers of the Forward areas have been disposed of as ordered by Astrend.	Anne

WAR DIARY
or
INTELLIGENCE SUMMARY.
(Erase heading not required.)

Army Form C. 2118.

140 Field Amb. 101

Place	Date 1917 Sept	Hour	Summary of Events and Information	Remarks and references to Appendices
Voormezeele	24		Parties from the arrived during night, last party arrived 6.30am. All Officers & men relieved from the line, handed over all clearing stores etc to relief party at Voormezeele, also obtained all the receipts from the C.P. & O.P. Heard that Hedge St was blown in by a shell & Capt Dunlop buried, suffering from Shock. Confusion was encountered. 16 horses 5 trap horse lines had wagons parked, men embussed. Transport to follow. To report to A.D.M.S. at Caestre, arrived in car at mid-day, was given a map & opened for 2 farms near Hondegheni, left man to meet Transport to follow. Arrived at our assigned billets, admission strenuously refused, left car & was shown their billet returned to A.D.M.S. office to report, went to Div H.Q. & St Sulle's given as Q.33.b. central, was able to stop transport at Caestre, sent them both farm & orders to go on.	
Caestre (Q.33 B Central)	25		Conference of C.Os at A.D.M.S. Office. Was informed that the blockage at Larch Wood & dock of individuals. Went on to B.H.Q (1.24.8 Regd) arranged about busses & shifting for our move to 14 Army th. In the evening a message that I am to report to reserve Infantry S.O.S received A.D.M.S. office	

Army Form C. 2118.

WAR DIARY
or
INTELLIGENCE SUMMARY.
(Erase heading not required.)

Instructions regarding War Diaries and Intelligence Summaries are contained in F. S. Regs., Part II. and the Staff Manual respectively. Title pages will be prepared in manuscript.

140 Field Amb: 11/

Place	Date 1917 Septem[ber]	Hour	Summary of Events and Information	Remarks and references to Appendices
Caestre (Q33 b.enl)	26th		Interviewed the General with the A.D.M.S, offered my defence, was told to return & see the General C.D.C. 41st Division) at 12 noon, which I did. He told me that he was satisfied that though there had been a temporary blockage the evacuation of wounded generally was carried out well, that this matter as far as he was concerned was ended, & that the report had been destroyed, that it would not stand against me in the future. Colonel reviewed that our transport move with R.Coh tomorrow morning to Wormhoudt & from there on 28th to Ghyvelde – & Army. We followed by Bus on 28th. Mail well. received any arrangements.	Annexure three
"	27th		Transport moved up to Wormhoudt under Capt. Davidson & Butler. Called at 104 R.H.Q.	three
"	28		Men marched to Bevre to entrain at 7 a.m. Collected 3 sick from Regt. Came by car via Cassel, Bergues & Dunkirk to Ghyvelde, then in billets. School as Hqrs to accommodate 20 sick. Mqrs in front of Church & Hosp. in some way. In the evening bombed by hostile planes, 2 killed & 12 wounded on the line. H.Q. mess. Capts. Rocheford, Butler, Lt. Harvey & 70 men to go to Corps Rest Stat. tomorrow.	three
Ghyvelde	29th		Unpacking, kit inspection equip. Party left for Corps Rest Station. Sent in S/Sgt. Talbot, Cpl. Savage & Taylor for New Year Honours. A.D.M.S. called.	three

WAR DIARY
or
INTELLIGENCE SUMMARY

(Erase heading not required.)

Army Form C. 2118

14.0 Field Amb.

Place	Date	Hour	Summary of Events and Information	Remarks and references to Appendices
Ghyvelde	1917 Sept. 30th		O.C.'s conference at ADMS. La Plane. Instructions at this A.S.O. Staring parade to form an orderly order. Many of the clothes much destroyed by work in the tent, + kits lost. Madge St. All being indented for to complete. J. M. Tilson Lt. Col. RAMC O.C. 140 F. Amb.	A
			Attached (1) A = Scheme of Evacuation (2) B = Inf. O.C. on transf. from O.O. of Lt Bouchvier & See.	

DIAGRAM SHOWING LINE OF EVACUATION OF CASUALTIES.

Legend: ── Seriously Wounded. ══ Walking Wounded.

Responsibility for evacuation — O.C. 139th Field Amb. for Wounded ; A.C.P.
" " Left Bde. — Capt. Chaney, 14th R.A.P.
" " Right " — Capt. Davidson, 16th F.A.P. Advanced Collecting Post.

FRONT LINE.

- Left Brigade: 14th R.A.P., No.2 R.A.P., J.25 a 2.2, J.30 b 2.8
- Right Brigade: No.3 R.A.P., No.4 R.A.P., J.30 a 9.8, J.30 a 4.4
- Bersey Walk — Hedge St. J.30 b 2.8
- Clemsons Lane — Canada St. J.30 a 4.4
- Birch Wood — Collecting Post — Tramline & Track
- Advanced Collecting Post

A.D.M.S. 41st Division
No. S.724.

Circulated to each Brigade Headquarters, C.R.A.,
C.R.E. etc, Officers Commanding Units and all
Medical Officers.

11 Sept. 1917.

B

Operation Orders 140 Field Ambulance.   Copy No.1.

19 Sep: 1917.

General. All general information regarding Boundaries, Objectives, Tracks, Headquarters etc. for the coming Offensive is included in the Medical arrangements of this Division as issued by the A.D.M.S.

1. The 140 Field Ambulance will evacuate the Line with Transport in field near VOORMEZEELE

  Headquarters.   VOORMEZEELE
  Advanced Dressing Station   LOCK 8   I.32 a 8·5
  Collecting Post   LARCH WOOD   I.29 c 2·7
  Advanced Collecting Posts   Hedge Street   for Left Brigade.   I.30 b 2·8
                CANADA STREET for Right Brigade.   I.30 - 4·2

2. **Regimental Aid Posts.**   For Left Brigade.   No 1. CLONMEL COPSE   J.19 c 4·3
                    No 2. ILIAD LANE.   J.25 a 3·8
            For Right Brigade.   No 3 } ILIAD AVENUE   I.30 b 9·3
                    No 4 }

3. **Evacuations**

  (a) To R.A.P's 1.2.3. and 4. by Regimental Stretcher Bearers. The attention of all is directed to 41 Div No A 29/115 and to para (4) b. of ADMS Medical arrangements issued under ADMS S510 do 20·4·17.

  (b) From R.A.P's 1 and 2 to Advanced Collecting Post. HEDGE STREET. By duckboard track TOWSEY TRACK by R.A.M.C.

  From R.A.P's 3 and 4 to Advanced Collecting Post. CANADA STREET. By duckboard track CLEMSON'S LANE by R.A.M.C.

  (c) From Advanced Collecting Posts to COLLECTING POST, LARCH WOOD. By tramline and track.

  (d) From Collecting Post LARCH WOOD to ADVANCE DRESSING STATION LOCK 8.

  (a) By tramline. (b) By track. (c) By wheeled stretcher track to VERBRANDEN ROAD at about I.28 b 5·2. thence by Motor Ambulance direct to CORPS MAIN DRESSING STATION. via VOORMEZEELE.

  (d) Corps Light Railway running at stated hours to be notified later. Will take WALKING WOUNDED direct to REMY SIDING.

4. **Classification and Distribution of Wounded.** All casualties will be divided into

  (1) Seriously Wounded - lying & sitting cases.
  (2) Walking Cases.

at the Collecting Post. LARCH WOOD and Advanced Dressing station at LOCK 8, and distributed as follows :-

Classt sent either direct by Motor Ambulance from LARCH WOOD to CORPS Main Dressing

Station for seriously wounded CHIPPEWA M6 a 8·8. or by Tramline to Advanced Dressing Station LOCK 8. and thence by Motor Ambulance to CHIPPEWA.

Class 2. to Corps Main Dressing for Walking Wounded - either :-

(1) by CORPS LIGHT RAILWAY. — to REMY.

(2) by Track to Advanced Dressing Station LOCK 8. and thence by Lorry or Horse Ambulance.

(3) by Horse Ambulance or lorry direct from LARCH WOOD.

<u>Distribution of Wounded.</u> (1) Lightly Wounded. (Including Prisoners of War + Self Inflicted) and slightly sick to LA CLYTTE.

(2) All Seriously Wounded - including Prisoners of War - moribund, gas and seriously sick to CHIPPEWA. M6 a 8·8.

6. <u>Responsibility of Command.</u> The O.C 140 F.A. is responsible for the Advanced Collecting Posts, Collecting Post, Advanced Dressing Station and VOORMEZEELE. and the evacuation from the Advanced Collecting Posts to the CORPS MAIN DRESSING STATIONS. and will take steps to see that these Posts and Dressing Stations are stocked with Medical, Surgical, and Ordnance Supplies etc. CAPTAIN CHESNEY. MC, RAMC. will be Officer in charge forward bearers and is responsible for the evacuation from R.A.P's 1 and 2 to the Advanced Collecting Posts, HEDGE STREET. He will maintain 'liason' with the M.O's i/c Units in that Area, assist in establishment of further R.A.P's further forward. and help the Regimental medical Establishments as much as possible. He will be responsible that his Aid Posts are duly equipped. Headquarters HEDGE STREET.

CAPTAIN DAVIDSON RAMC. will fulfil a similar function with similar responsibilities evacuating R.A.P's 3 and 4. to CANADA STREET. Headquarters CANADA STREET. Officers in charge . Forward Bearers must make themselves thoroughly acquainted with the area for which they are responsible - both forwards + backwards.

7. <u>Distribution of Personnel.</u>

<u>Officers</u>. Special dispositions Advanced Coll. Post. HEDGE STREET . CAPT. E.A. LUMLEY. in charge
       do   CANADA STREET. CAPT. J.S DOYLE "
       do   LARCH WOOD   CAPT. LAUDER "

All the above Officers are under the command of O.C 140 F.A.

<u>Personnel.</u> (a) Two Bearer Sub divs. 138 F.A. for O/c Forward Bearers HEDGE STREET
  (b)   do   140 F.A   do   do   CANADA STREET
  (c) One Bearer Sub div 138 F.A. fr. Ad: Coll: Post HEDGE STREET for evac: to LARCH WOOD
  (d)   do   140 F.A   do   CANADA STREET
  (e) Two bearer Sub. div. 139 F.A. at disposal of O.C 140 F.A.

Each bearer sub division thus placed at the disposal of O.C. this Fd. Amb.

Forward bearers to be complete to War Establishment (less Officers) and accompanied by Stretchers.

8. **Distribution of Officers.**

	O/C for Bearers	HEDGE ST.	CANADA ST.	LARCH WOOD	LOCK 8	VOORMEZEELE	L.H. DEPOT
138 F.A	1	1		3			3
139 F.A.	-	-	-	-	-	1	
140 F.A.	1	2	1	-	1	2	

	O.R.S.
138 F.A	3
139 F.A	-
140 F.A	-

9. **Transport.**

(a) *Motor Ambulances*. All Motor Ambulances will be placed at the disposal of O.C. 140 F.A. with the exception of one Motor Amb: to be retained by O.C. of O.R.S.

(b) *Horse Ambulances and G.S. Wagons*. Will likewise be placed at disposal of O.C. 140 F.A. G.S. Wagons should be fitted up ready to take sitting cases.

(c) *Wheeled Stretchers*. Wheeled Stretchers from 138 and 139 Bty's will be placed at disposal of this F.A.

(d) Three Lorries will be allotted to O.C. 140 F.A. under Corps arrangement.

10. **Casualty Clearing Stations** at GODEWAERSVELDE and are No. 11, 37 & 41 C.C.S.

11. **Records.** Admission and Discharge Books will not be kept at either Collecting Posts or Advanced Dressing Stations. Nominal Rolls (in duplicate) will be kept at LARCH WOOD, LOCK 8, and VOORMEZEELE. To reach this Office by 5:0 pm daily.

Situation Reports will be forwarded daily by O/C Forward Bearers to this Office.

12. **Telephones.** LARCH WOOD COLLECTING POST, LOCK 8 A.D.S. at VOORMEZEELE, will be linked to H.Q. 41 Div.

13. **Field Medical Cards.** Field Medical Cards must be issued to patients at LARCH WOOD, who are sent to REMY SIDING. They must bear the Fd. Ambulance Stamp. The word "Received" will be printed on top and under it written "No A.T.S." All Light Cases sent to REMY will be entered in the A&D Book & included in usual returns.

14. **Trollies** Distribution of.
CANADA STREET and HEDGE STREET = 6 each
LARCH WOOD = 9
LOCK 8 = 3
VOORMEZEELE = 3

13. **Rations** Rations will be apportioned and labelled clearly for LOCK 8, LARCH WOOD, CANADA ST, FORWARD BEARERS DITTO, HEDGE ST, FORWARD BEARERS DITTO. This division will take place at VOORMEZEELE, sufficient allowance must be made for patients at LARCH WOOD.

SGT SLAWSON at LARCH WOOD will be responsible for the forward distribution of these rations, and will obtain receipts for all rations distributed from LARCH WOOD.

                                                            [signature]
                                                            Lt. Col. RAMC
Issued at 15-45 hrs   O.C. 140 Field Ambulance.
19 September 1917.

Copy No 1 File
    2 War Diary.
    3 A.D.M.S 41 Div.
    4 O.C 138 Fd. Amb.
    5 O.C 139 Fd. Amb.
    6 Capt J.La?. Lauder, D.S.O., M.C., RAMC.
    7. Capt J.P. Davidson. R.A.M.C.

Redistribution of Stretcher Bearers/detachments 5. See para.

Marked _____ given for time between detachments &
Mode of Evacuation 6. At 12 hr. 2 detachment of bearers
(1st line) move forward to reinforce those at ADS
there will be bearers (in the field) under command
of Capt HOGG. (one detachment to each sector)

(2) at 2½ hrs (3rd line) & 2 detachment
of bearers 3rd line (2nd line 1st 1st line) return
to rest. (one detachment to each sector)

(3) after that bearers will be changed
every 2 hrs — 4 detachments in the line and
2 in rest — giving 8 hrs on duty, 4 hrs o/o.

2° Dump 7. At CARLTON TRENCH at 22 ___ a 2°
dump for wounded will be formed at
ORCHARD TRENCH. (called ORCHARD Dump)

EVACUATION of ADS under paragraph 8. With relays of bearers
to "Post"

EVACUATION of the wounded / 2° Dump called ORCHARD Dump
9. will be 2 detachments from front to ORCHARD DUMP
" 2 " " ORCHARD DUMP &
GREEN DUMP. The last detachment is always
carrying on from front line of evacuation.

Copy No 1 File   R. C. _____
      2 WAR DIARY   Major (_____)
      3 Capt HOGG.

4. The 140th Field Ambulance will parade at 1.30 pm on 3rd October in full marching order, worn helmets, and water bottles filled ready to march out.

All wagons will be packed and bivouacs & bivouac tents will be carried to the new bivouac area.

5. ROUTE.
Fairweather track N of DERNANCOURT — MEAULTE — FRICOURT road — MAMETZ to X 29 d.

6. Captain ROWBOTHAM will conduct the parade & will report to O.C. the Field Ambulance at X 29 d on arrival.

Copy No 1 File
    2 War diary
    3 Capt Rowbotham
    4. Transport Officer

R C Wilmot
Major
OC 140 F Amb

Issued at 10.30 am
Handed personally

140th Field Ambulance. Operation Order No 2
Copy No 2

Ref Maps   57c. SW 1/20.000
                57c   1/40.000
                57d   1/40.000

Information.

1 (a) The 41st Division will continue the offensive at Zero hour on 7th October, and will establish a line through M18 central. N13 central to LIGNY – THILLOY Road.

(b) Brigade Headquarters.
    124 Inf Bde.   S 6 a.8.7 (FERRET TRENCH)
    122 Inf Bde.   M 30 c 3.5 : 0.5.
    123 Inf Bde.   CARLTON TRENCH.

(c) 139 and 140 Field Ambulance bearers with 32 infantry men from each of 122 and 123 J.B will be under command of O.C 139 Field Ambulance and will carry out evacuation of the wounded.

138 Field Ambulance bearers and 32 bearers 124 J.B will be in reserve at MEDICAL DUMP under the orders of the A.D.M.S.

Instruction. 2.

(a) Captain ROWBOTHAM 140 Field Ambulance with 12 bearers 140 Field Ambulance
and 32 O.Ranks 122 J.B
and 32 O.Ranks 123 J.B
all with skeleton kits and ground sheets will proceed to THISTLE ALLEY (S16 4.3) at 4.30am arriving at THISTLE ALLEY at 6.0 am. Under command of O.C 139 F.A from this time.

140 Field Ambulance Operation Order by Capt...
Aug 1917

Information

1. (a) The attack... [faded]
   ... Bn will establish a line through
   ... RIBECY – TRIANGLE Post

   Objective dispositions

   ... Bde ... S.A. Bty (Right) (North)
   ... Bde ... T.M. Bty (Left)
   ... Bn ... SACKVILLE TRENCH

   (b) ... Bde will advance with 2 infantry
   ...battalions in line supported with one mixed (reserve)
   ... reserve will support the 2nd infantry

   (c) ... Field Ambulance will open stretcher
   bearers and 32 bearers 124 7.13
   will be in reserve at MEDICAL DUMP under the orders
   of the A.D.M.S.

Instructions 2.

(a) Captain ROWBOTHAM 140 Field Ambulance with 12 bearers
    140 Field Ambulance
    and 32 O.Ranks 122 3.13
    and 32 O.Ranks 125 3.13
    all with stretcher kits and ground sheets will proceed to
    THISTLE ALLEY (Sh 43) at 4.30am arriving at
    THISTLE ALLEY at 6.0 am. Under command of O.C. 123
    F.A. from this time.

(b) Lieut ROCHE 138 Field Ambulance will accompany the party as far as FLAT IRON COPSE and will report to O.C 139 F.Amb. for duty there.

(c) Sergt Sawyer will also accompany the party as far as FLAT IRON COPSE and report to O.C 139 F.Amb. for duty in connection with regulating transport there.

(d) Sgt Major ASC 139 Fd Amb with 2 G.S Wagons (each with 4 H.D horses) from each 138, 139 and 140 Fd Ambulances and 1 water cart (with 4 Mules) of 140 Fd Ambulance will accompany the party to FLAT IRON COPSE and report to O.C 139 Fd. Ambulance there. He will take rations for the animals.

(e) Rations for personnel will be obtained at FLAT IRON COPSE for all; those proceeding further up the line obtaining them en route.

(f) Iron Helmets, iron rations and 2 Gas Helmets will be worn by all ranks.

(g) Water Bottles will be carried full by all.

(h) Care will be taken to see that no documents etc indicating the unit to which men belong are carried.

Reports. 3

To O/C 139 Fd. Ambulance under whose orders all become on arrival at their destination.

Zero hour 1.45 pm.

Copy No 1 File.
   2 War Diary
   3 A.D.M.S by S.R.
   4 Capt. Rowbotham } handed personally.
   5 Transport Officer 140 Fd.Amb.

Oct 6th 1916
Issued at 8.55 pm

R.C Wilmot
Major
OC 140 F Amb

140th Field Ambulance Operation Order No 10

Copy No 2

Ref maps 57D 1/40,000
     62D 1/40,000

1. Information (a) The 41st Division will be relieved by the 30th Division on the 10/11th October.
   (b) The relief of medical units will be completed by 10am 11th October.
   (c) 140th Field Ambulance will take over CORPS COLLECTING STATION for Walking Wounded at BÉCORDEL.

2. Instructions (a) The Main body will proceed in full marching order. Parade 8.30 am 11th October OC in Command
   (b) The Rear Party as detailed with Transport under command Captain Hobson will pack wagons, strike tents and be prepared to move at 10 am on relief by the Field Ambulance of 30th Division.
   (c) All patients will be seen by the Orderly officer and those fit returned to their units. The remainder will be sent by motor ambulance to CORPS REST STATION or CCS according to their severity.
   (d) All ambulance wagons Horse & Motor will proceed to CORPS collecting STATION BÉCORDEL.
   (e) All bivouacs will be left for inspection.

3. ROUTE. MAMETZ – FRICOURT Road to
F4 central (?) by MARICOURT –
BÉCORDEL Road. Tramway (?) track
will be used where possible.

4. REPORTS to CORPS COLLECTING STATION
for WALKING WOUNDED BÉCORDEL
after 10 a.m. October 11th.

Copy No 1 File
       2 War Diary
       3 A.D.M.S. (?)
       4 Capt Roberts handed personally

Oct 10th 1916
Issued at 12.10 p.m.   R.E. Howard (?)
                                 Major
                              Senior (?) P.M.O (?)

140º Field Ambulance – Operation Order No 11.
CORPS COLLECTING STATION for WALKING WOUNDED

Copy No 2

Information
1. The XV Corps will attack at 2.15 p.m to-day, and walking wounded may be expected from 4 p.m onwards in considerable numbers.

Instructions. 2.
At 4 p.m. Lt CONNOLLY will assist Lt DAVIES in the Dressing Tent and two extra dressers will be provided.

At the same hour Capt: ROWBOTHAM will take over the duties of distributing officer.

Lieut: ROCHE will take over the duties of distributing officer from Capt ROWBOTHAM at 12 midnight 12/13ᵗʰ.

Capt HOGG will relieve Lieut DAVIES at 9.0 pm in the dressing tent

and LIEUT. DAVIES will relieve Lieut CONNOLLY at 3 am 13ᵗʰ and Lieut: CONNOLLY Capt HOGG at 9 a.m.

Capt ROWBOTHAM will relieve Lieut ROCH at 8 p.m.

After this, reliefs will proceed at 6 hrs interval in the dressing tent, and at 8 hrs interval in the distributing shed for officers, until normal conditions are resumed.

DRESSING TENT OFFICERS.
Capt. HOGG
Lieut DAVIES
"   CONNOLLY

Distributing Officers
    CAPTAIN   ROWBOTHAM
    Lieut.   RUCH.

3. N.C.O's and Men continue reliefs as before and those resting may be called upon in emergency.

Oct 12th - 1916

R C Wilmot
    Major RAMC
Commanding 140 Field Ambulance

Copy No 1   File
     2   War Diary
     3   ADMS
     4   Officers Notice Board.

Issued at 3.17 p.m.

Copy No 2

140th Field Ambulance Operation Order No 12
Oct 18th 1916

1. <u>Information</u>. The Field Ambulance will move to 2nd Army Area by rail on October 19th.

2. <u>Parade</u>. Transport at 2.30 pm
   Personnel at 4.30 pm
   opp to Mill at BETTENCOURT.

3. <u>Route</u>

4. <u>Motor ambulances</u> will proceed to LONGPRE Station leaving at 5 pm. Captain ROWBOTHAM will be in command of the convoy. They will proceed on departure of the train via VIGNACOURT - DOULLENS - St POL - ANVIN - ST HILAIRE - AIRE - HAZEBROUCK - FLETRE

5. <u>Rations</u> for day of entraining will be carried on the person as well as the unexpired portion of the day's ration.

6. The <u>Supply wagon</u> will entrain with the unit with supplies for 20th inst.

7. <u>Breast ropes</u> for entraining horses will be arranged for by the Transport Officer. Harness will be taken off animals & packed in sacks in the centre of the truck.

Care will be taken to 'sand' the floors of the horse trucks, if sand or any suitable material is available.

8. REPORTS. to BETTENCOURT at 4.30 pm 19th inst & after at LISBURKE station.

9. Departure. Train departs for new body at 18 ish. One two horse ambulance wagon will leave. Train departs at 22.11 hrs with two horse ambulance wagon with team.

Copy, No. 1 File
2 War Diary
3 A.D.M.S
4. 124 Inf. Bde.

Rawland?

Brigade HQrs.

Ref Maps 5a 7a 28 & 7b   Oct 22" 1916   Copy No 2

140th Field Ambulance Operation Order No 13.

1. The 140th Field Ambulance will relieve the 1st Australian Field Ambulance. Relief to be completed by 6am October 24th 1916.

2. Dispositions.

   "A" Section less Captain Davies and permanent staff will take over the Baths & Laundry at RENINGHELST.
   Captain R.W. HOGG in command.

   "B" Section will take over the evacuation from the aid posts at SHRAPNEL ?? (I.29.a.3.?) and VIERSTRAAT (I.31.?.5.?) to the main dressing station at OUDE CHAM (G.30.?.4.?) the former via BEDFORD HOUSE and the latter via DICKEBUSCH A.D.S.
   Captain E.D. ROWBOTHAM in command.

   "C" Section with two officers will take over the Main Dressing Station at RENINGHELST.
   Captain J.P. DAVIDSON in command.

3. Captain DAVIDSON will detail the undermentioned personnel from C Section as Motor orderlies they will relieve the men at present employed by the Australian Field Ambulance.

   RENINGHELST ....
   DICKEBUSCH ....
   VIERSTRAAT ....

There are some extra cases for description
& accommodation but continue to be patients
by the Field Ambulance.
Relief to be completed on 22 October.

3. **Advance Party**
OC's Evacuation, Bath, and Main Dressing
Station RENINGHELST will arrange for the necessary
personnel & equipment to proceed to the
respective commanders on 22.25.

4. Main Body will parade at ____ on ____

5. Divisional Rest Station ____ and ____ NOVEMBER Lts 1.

6. On relief being completed the unit less advanced
will evacuate the life cases of the divisional front,
3 battalions of 123 Inf Bde in the line — Brigade
Headquarters BURGOMASTERS House

7. **REPORTS**
Reports after 8am 22 Oct at G. RENINGHELST.

Copy No 1 File
— 2 War Diary
— 3 OC 'B' Section
— 4 OC 'C' Section
— 5 OC Bath Captain ____
— 6 ADMS
— 7 123 Inf Bde
Issued at 11.25 am

War Diary

140 Field Ambulance.

OCTOBER 1917.

COMMITTEE FOR THE
MEDICAL HISTORY OF THE WAR
Date 8 DEC. 1917

Army Form C. 2118.

WAR DIARY
or
INTELLIGENCE SUMMARY.
(Erase heading not required.)

Vol. XVIII

140 Field Amb. (1)

Instructions regarding War Diaries and Intelligence Summaries are contained in F. S. Regs., Part II. and the Staff Manual respectively. Title pages will be prepared in manuscript.

Place	Date	Hour	Summary of Events and Information	Remarks and references to Appendices
	October 1917			
Chyvelde	1		Camps billets & Hospital as before. Hostile planes bombing at night.	Appx
"	2		Went to Indycote & saw the C.O. of the Corps Rest-station, re his sharing some of my men to attend A/Bhi's Inspection. He regretted he could not spare them.	Appx
"	3		Attend Inspection of Devisional Transport, Hospital, Camp & Baths. Men in marching order. Was afterwards complimented on the good work they had done in the recent offensive. Our wagons were not satisfactory arranged with the right same. Went on 10 days leave, handed over to Capt Davidson, as Capt Rowland is at the Corps Rest-station. Warning orders received in afternoon to be prepared to move to Teteghem, all steps taken. Order cancelled in evening	Appx
"	4		Warning orders received re move on by H. to De Groote Kwinte Farm. Personnel continuing sand bagging of transport lines. C.O.C. Division & May. Gen Jeugel G.B. visited transport lines.	Appx
"	6		Advanced party to De Groote Farm. There have been Hung Guns shelling " Very	Appx
"	7		Marched 9.30am for De Groote Farm arrived 12.30pm very wet & blustery. Orders to collect -	Appx
De Groote Kwinte Farm		12.30pm	Sick from 122 Bgde. Lt. (A.M.) Wright returned from leave. Changed Summer to Winter Time.	

Army Form C. 2118.

WAR DIARY
or
INTELLIGENCE SUMMARY.
(Erase heading not required.)

140th Field Amb.

Place	Date	Hour	Summary of Events and Information	Remarks and references to Appendices
De Groote Kunne Farm.	October 1917 8th		Cars sent to collect sick from 122 Bgde, no sick, they had been collected by 139 F.A.	
			Men employed washing wagons & started painting Horse Amb. Capt Davidson visited Div's collection of sick, orders to collect sick of 122 Bgde, to send bag huts down	AMC
"	9th		Sandbagging & painting continued.	AMC
"	10th		Horse Amb removed, about sunset	
"	11th		Capt Doyle left for temporary duty 21st K.R.R. to relieve Capt Bain proceeding on leave	AMC
			Capt Jardine posted to this Ambulance & sent to XI Corps for duty.	
			O.P. orders received, re move to St Idesbalde to take over from 139 F. Amb.	AMC
			Capt Davidson rd to 15/397 Q. to settle points in taking over at St Idesbalde	AMC
12th		11.40am	Bus wanted with view to taking over this future.	
	13		Sent advanced party to St Idesbalde. Advanced party arrived here at 7.40 p.m. (ordering)	
			from 113 F. Lane F.A. This Amb. handed over left 9 gun arrived 3 p.m. Artill.	
St Idesbalde			Over from 139 F.A. at St Idesbalde. Capt Blake (J.J.) arrived for duty in	
			place of Capt Rostron who is leaving this Ambulance. Arrival of the	
			following Mobel with following to gallant conduct in the field. St Sgt Bishop, L/Cpl Reedy, Pte Ballenger	MMM
			Newton, Cook, Barton, Millet, Nickel, Cpl Richardson	

Instructions regarding War Diaries and Intelligence Summaries are contained in F. S. Regs., Part II. and the Staff Manual respectively. Title pages will be prepared in manuscript.

WAR DIARY
or
INTELLIGENCE SUMMARY.
(Erase heading not required.)

Army Form C. 2118.

(3)

140 Field Amb

Place	Date 1917 October	Hour	Summary of Events and Information	Remarks and references to Appendices
St. Idesbalde	14th		Men in large hut, Hospital good Belgian hut capable of holding about 60 cases. Instructed to retain no case over 48 hrs, then send on to Corps Rest Station, arrangements to collect from Coast defences, & support Bde, also local sick. Personnel started sand bagging of huts. ADMS held board 6.30 pm. Capt Rowland returned from C.R.S. Capt Clarke relieved him.	[illegible]
"	15th		Capt Rowland left Amb. to report to [illegible] Amb. [illegible] for duty. I am very sorry to lose this officer.	[illegible]
"	16th		I returned from leave & took over from Capt Lawton. Camp shelled with H.E. from 8.30 pm off & on all night, several houses hit, 1 [illegible] killed, 3 or 4 cases of wounded. Men sandbagging & painting all day.	
"	18th		Sandbagging, & painting wagons. DADMS [illegible] reference to huts for [illegible] treatment of trench feet, hut fixed on, necessary [illegible], Began building [illegible]. Capt [illegible] sent up to Ave Capelle to take Capt [illegible] duty for one night.	
"	19th		Capt Lawton on duty to see the [illegible]	
"	20th		I held P.B. board for A [illegible]. Continuing painting of wagons, building [illegible] & checking Mob. Equip. Difficulty in getting trough [illegible] of the French [illegible]	

A6945 Wt. W11422/M1160 350,000 12/16 D. D. & L. Forms/C./2118/14.

WAR DIARY
or
INTELLIGENCE SUMMARY

(Erase heading not required.)

Army Form C. 2118.

140 Field Amb.

Place	Date 1917 October	Hour	Summary of Events and Information	Remarks and references to Appendices
S'Idesbalde	22"		Saw RPS. re material for the hut. To reach feet the diggers of the pits for waste water etc. In viewing one of our planes flying to observer Hun, one possibly with a inclined failure (to Ryan & Smith) Capt. Butler went on leave.	
"	23		The Rev. Father CRC went on leave. Officers - we are sending 6 men every 3rd day.	AM
"	24"		Sandbagging hut lines, putting up wind screens to huns, drew 2 Henry Huses, pulled (...) mess	AM
"	26		Still unable to get the troughs, benches, etc. to second feed-hut, have drummed all the other necessaries, two men in hospital at present, one car from 139 F.A. Shells in	PM
"	28"		Orders at 9. a.m. from HW. proper an hour's move, we are attached to 122 Brigade, moved with them to the necessary steps. Over 40 men returned from CRS. in the evening. Also 2 officers attending QL.O.O from 122 Buffs transpt. moving Arm to Fort Mardick 7th. Sh.H.mak Pneumonia	PM
"	29"		Personal embus. ADW. party from S. African Units (G.M.Blis) arrived totals over 90 men, sick, Pers.not under Capt. Donaldson by 4pm. Hundred over to incoming units. Personnel embused about 3.30 pm, transport under Capt. Donaldson by 6 pm.	Fluid
Fort Mardick		4:30 pm	Hd.Q. etc. to unit arrived Fort Mardick about 3 pm. Shelbergue about 17 miles via Dunkirk Rooms arranged sleeping. 6:30 pm Men in good health. No Hospital 5 sick and a return collected from B.G.O.L in the evening Report received M.Brens (Mole-les-Bains) & B.G.A.122. Pt. Breen saw missing when we entrained	Pt.H

A6945 Wt. W11422/M1160 350,000 12/16 D. D. & L. Forms/C./2118/14.

Army Form C. 2118.

WAR DIARY
or
INTELLIGENCE SUMMARY.

(Erase heading not required.)

140 Field Amb

Place	Date	Hour	Summary of Events and Information	Remarks and references to Appendices
	1917 Oct			(5)
Fort Marduck	30th	2am	Received from "A" offices through D.D.A.S instructions re Commencing of Nibo + certain material carried on and dated 28" . Issued orders accordingly. Went over arrangements. Obtained material. Sent D.M.& D.A.D.O.S. for clothing together outstanding indents, only able to get very little done	
	31st		To HQ and office CO. Conference 11 am. Col. Rattray morning & Col. Strong afternoon, CRE. H.O. my Fwd. C.S. in the Cavalry Field Amb. taking over as Estmt. Collected necessary sups. Capt Butler as indents for stores, clothing, dressing etc. making necessary steps. Returned from Front about hds. inspection 10.30am the Section Officers inspected myself at 3 pm all clothing stores to pay and necessary in town lay Kirkuk.	J W Ashton Lieut Colonel O.C. 140 F.A.

www.ingramcontent.com/pod-product-compliance
Lightning Source LLC
Chambersburg PA
CBHW081529160426

43191CB00011B/1717